ACTION PHILOSOPHERS!

The lives and thoughts of history's A-list brain trust told in a hip and humorous fashion

by Fred Van Lente and Ryan Dunlavey

ROLL CALL for ACTION!!

"PHILOSOPHY IS NOT A THEORY, BUT AN ACTIVITY."
--LUDWIG WITTGENSTEIN,
TRACTATUS LOGICO-PHILOSOPHICUS

ACTION PHILOSOPHERS GIANT-SIZE THING VOL. 1 IS PUBLISHED BY EVIL TWIN COMICS, 262 FIFTH AVENUE, 2ND FLOOR, BROOKLYN NY, 11215. THE MATERIAL IN THIS BOOK ORIGINALLY APPEARED IN PERIODICAL FORM IN ACTION PHILOSOPHERS #1-3. ALL CONTENTS ARE COPYRIGHT AND TRADEMARKED 2006 BY RYAN DUNLAVEY AND FRED VAN LENTE. ALL RIGHTS RESERVED. NO PART OF THIS PUBLICATION MAY BE REPRODUCED WITHOUT WRITTEN PERMISSION FROM THE COPYRIGHT HOLDERS. FIRST PRINTING: JUNE 2006. PRINTED IN CANADA.

THE FIRST SIX STORIES IN THIS BOOK WERE ORIGINALLY MADE POSSIBLE WITH A GENEROUS GRANT FROM THE XERIC FOUNDATION. (WWW.XERICFOUNDATION.COM)

ISBN #0-9778329-0-2

PLATO!!!

"PLATO" MEANS "*BROAD*" OR "*FLAT*" AND WAS THE *STAGE NAME* OF A *PRO WRESTLER* BORN *ARISTOCLES* ON THE ISLAND OF *AEGINA* IN 428 B.C.!

APPARENTLY HE ADOPTED THIS *NOM DE GUERRE* BECAUSE OF HIS EXCEPTIONALLY BROAD *SHOULDERS.**

*: YES, *REALLY.*

THOUGH TWO-TIME CHAMP OF THE *ISTHMIAN GAMES*, PLATO NEVER QUALIFIED FOR THE *OLYMPICS*, NECESSITATING A *CAREER SWITCH.*

PLATO'S MIGHTY HEART *BREAKING*...

CLOSED

YOU SUCK

WHILE DABBLING IN POETRY AND POLITICS IN *ATHENS,* MR. BROAD FELL IN WITH THE WANDERING SAGE *SOCRATES* AND HIS YOUTHFUL STUDENTS.

SOCRATES GOT INTO THE *PHILOSOPHY* RACKET WHEN FAMED "PSYCHIC FRIEND" *THE ORACLE AT DELPHI* TOLD HIM...

NO MAN IS AS WISE AS *SOCRATES!*

CALL NOW! ONLY $3.⁹⁹/MINUTE

1-900-4 ORACLE

COOL!

HE WENT ABOUT *PROVING* THIS BY SHOOTING DOWN ATHENIAN CONVENTIONAL WISDOM IN BACK-AND-FORTH *"DIALECTIC"* CRITIQUES:

SO IF *RELIGION* IS *B.S.,* THEN *YOU* TELL *ME:* WHAT *IS* TRUTH?

I DO NOT *KNOW.*

WHAT? THEN HOW CAN YOU BE WISER THAN *EVERYBODY ELSE?*

BECAUSE *I KNOW* THAT. I DO NOT KNOW.

BY ZEUS, YOU'RE A *PAIN IN THE ASS.*

SOCRATES ENCOURAGED HIS *STUDENTS* TO GET IN THE ACT, AND YOU KNOW HOW MUCH YOUNG PEOPLE *HATE* SHOWING UP THEIR *ELDERS:*...

IF YOU BOYS ARE SEARCHING FOR *TRUTH,* YOU SHOULD LOOK TO *ZEUS!*

ARE ZEUS'S ACTIONS *ARBITRARY,* OR IS *HE* GUIDED BY TRUTH TOO?

OF *COURSE* ZEUS IS GUIDED BY TRUTH!

WELL, IN THAT CASE, *I* SHOULD JUST LOOK FOR TRUTH...

...FOR A *WISE MAN* WOULD NOT *NEED* ZEUS!

>GASP! CHOKE!

PLATO WOULD CALL SOCRATES' DEATH THE TURNING POINT OF HIS LIFE.

ATHENS CITY LIMITS

BUT ATHENS WAS NO LONGER A SAFE PLACE FOR SOCRATIC STUDENTS! HE WANDERED THE MEDITERRANEAN WORLD IN EXILE FOR OVER A DECADE...

...FINALLY ENDING UP IN SICILY, WHERE HE ENCOUNTERED A SECT OF PYTHAGOREANS.

!?!

PYTHAGORAS—HE OF TRIANGLE THEOREM FAME—FOUNDED A BIZARRE CULT OF MATH HIPPIES IN THE 6TH CENTURY B.C. WHO BELIEVED THEY COULD COMPREHEND THE NATURE OF THE COSMOS THROUGH NUMBERS.

TO PURIFY THEIR MINDS FOR MYSTIC CALCULATIONS, THE PYTHAGOREANS TOOK A VOW OF SECRECY, COULD ONLY WEAR WHITE, AND SWORE OFF SEXUAL INTERCOURSE.

THAT LAST ONE >HEH!< SHOULDN'T BE MUCH OF A CHALLENGE!

SOME OF THE CULT'S *OTHER* TENETS WERE RATHER, ER, *UNIQUE...*
...LIKE A PROHIBITION AGAINST TOUCHING *BEANS.*

"*ALL IS NUMBER*" WAS THEIR WATCHWORD...

...MEANING OUR MESSY, MATERIAL UNIVERSE IS THE IMPERFECT *EXPRESSION* OF A HIGHER, ABSTRACT UNIVERSE...

...A *PERFECT* AND *HARMONIOUS* REALM OF *NUMBER.*

OHHHHH... REALM OF *NUMBERS...*

WAIT! PLATO KNOWS HE KNOW WHAT SOCRATES KNEW HE DID *NOT* KNOW!

WELL WHADAYA KNOW?

POOF!

EXPOSURE TO THIS THEORY LED PLATO TO THE CONCLUSION THAT *REAL* TRUTH WAS *ABSTRACT,* AND, LIKE NUMBERS UNCHANGING--*ETERNAL!*

ALL *CHAIRS,* FOR EXAMPLE, ARE SIMPLY THE *EXPRESSION* OF THE *IDEA* OF A CHAIR--AND THOUGH OUR "REAL" CHAIRS ARE FLAWED AND *TEMPORARY...*

FOR PLATO, THOUGH, THE HIGHEST DUTY OF THE PHILOSOPHER WAS TO LOOK *BEYOND* THESE SHADOWS OF OUR *PERCEIVED* REALITY...

...AND UNCOVER THE *FORMS* THAT *PROJECTED* THEM!

PLATO *SMASH!*

IN FACT, PREFERRING THE *IDEAL* TO THE *PHYSICAL* WAS *SUCH* AN OBSSESSION OF PLATO'S...

LAAAAANCE! I WANT OUR RELATIONSHIP TO STAY *PLATONIC!*

...THAT HIS *NAME* BECAME A *SYNONYM* FOR IT!

WHACK!

9

DIONYSIUS DECIDED TO *HUMILIATE* PLATO BY SELLING HIM INTO *SLAVERY* TO HIS HOMETOWN OF *AEGINA*, WHERE, FORTUITOUSLY, A BUDDY BOUGHT HIS FREEDOM.

PLATO DO *ANYTHING*, JUST DON'T WANT TO GET *REAL JOB!!*

LOT #42
1 Philosopher, Used.

HIS BENEFACTOR *ALSO* GAVE HIM ENOUGH DOUGH TO SET UP A *SCHOOL* JUST OUTSIDE ATHENS.

PLATO NAME IT AFTER FORMER RESIDENT OF *NEIGHBORHOOD*, HERO *HECADEMUS!*

AT THE ACADEMY PLATO DIVESTED PYTHAGORISM OF ITS *MONDO-BIZARRO* RITUALS...AND GAVE THE SOCRATICS' *KNEE-JERK CRITIQUING* THE THEORY OF FORMS AS AN OPERATING *VALUE SYSTEM*, THEREBY CREATING ...

...COLLEGE!

LIKE *ANY* GOOD PROFESSOR, PLATO *PUBLISHED* WIDELY AS WELL.

AGAIN?! BUT I GOTTA TALK ABOUT MY *INDEPENDENT STUDY!* >WHINE!<

OFFICE HOURS CANCELLED

PLATO'S WORKS TAKE THE FORM OF *DIALOGUES*, OR DISCUSSIONS BETWEEN TEACHER AND STUDENT. INVARIABLY THE *TEACHER* IS SOCRATES HIMSELF, *RESURRECTED* BY PLATO TO MOUTH *HIS OWN* THEORIES- AND GIVE THEM ADDED *LEGITIMACY!*

SOCRATES

BRAINS!! MUST...USE... *BRAINS!!*

PHILOSOPHY!
(SURPRISED?)

THESE PHILOSOPHER-RULERS WOULD *SLEEP TOGETHER*, WORK TOGETHER, AND SHARE *ALL POSSESSIONS*, AND *THIS* WOULD KEEP THEM FREE OF *CORRUPTION*.

(*POLITICAL* CORRUPTION, THAT IS.)

ONE OF THE 35 WOULD BE CHOSEN TO BE THE *PHILOSOPHER-KING* WHO WOULD RULE OVER *ALL*. ALL MUSIC AND LITERATURE THAT DID NOT PRAISE THE STATE WOULD BE *BANNED*—ALL *INDIVIDUALISM* WOULD BE UTTERLY *ERADICATED*.

PLATO WOULD HAVE FORCED *HUMAN SOCIETY* TO ADHERE TO THE *IMPOSSIBLE, ABSTRACT STANDARD* OF THE *REALM OF FORMS!*

IN 367 B.C. PLATO WAS OFFERED AN OPPORTUNITY TO *REALIZE* HIS DEMENTED BRAND OF *HOMOEROTIC FASCISM...*

DUDE! COME BACK TO SYRACUSE! MY BROTHER DIONYSUS IS DEAD! WE CAN SET UP *THE REPUBLIC*, IT'LL BE *AWESOME!*

HMMN...

YOU'RE AN *IDIOT*.

THINGS DIDN'T GO EXACTLY AS *PLANNED*. PLATO WISELY STAYED *OUT* OF POLITICS UNTIL HIS *DEATH* IN 347 B.C.

THE CHRISTIAN EMPEROR *JUSTINIAN* SHUT DOWN THE ACADEMY IN A.D. 529, BECAUSE IT WAS TOO *ATHEISTIC* FOR HIM. THIS EVENT IS USUALLY USED TO DEMARCATE THE START OF *THE DARK AGES*.

OUT OF BUSINESS

NEVERTHELESS, THE FUNDAMENTALS OF *ACADEMIC LIFE* HAVE CHANGED LITTLE SINCE PLATO *INVENTED* THEM...

HEY, KIDS! MEET ACTION PHILOSOPHER #2:
BODHIDHARMA!

...GRANDMASTER OF KUNG FU!!

THE *TIME?* A.D. *520!*

IF A TREE FALLS IN A FOREST AND *RYAN DUNLAVEY* ISN'T THERE TO DRAW IT AND *FRED VAN LENTE* ISN'T THERE TO SCRIPT IT, WILL IT MAKE A COMIC?

THE *PLACE?* THE *SHAOLIN* TEMPLE ATOP *SHAO-SHIH* MOUNTAIN IN RURAL *CHINA!*

HERE MONKS EMPLOY THEMSELVES TRANSLATING AND COPYING THE SACRED TEACHINGS OF BUDDHA, *THE ENLIGHTENED ONE...*

...FOUNDER OF THE RELIGION THAT EMERGED FROM *INDIA* IN THE 6TH CENTURY *B.C.* AND SWEPT *EAST,* BECOMING CHINA'S *NATIONAL* FAITH!

BUT THERE'S NOT A LOT OF *SCRIPTURE-COPYING* GOING ON *TODAY.*

TODAY *SHOULD* BE A *JOYFUL* DAY...

...FOR *BODHIDHARMA* HAS ARRIVED IN CHINA!

THE FAMED PATRIARCH OF THE *DHYANA SCHOOL* OF BUDDHISM DECIDED TO BECOME A POOR MISSIONARY, PREACHING IN FOREIGN LANDS, UPON THE DEATH OF HIS *OWN* TEACHER.

RUMOR HAD IT THAT HE WAS BORN TO VAST *WEALTH* IN CONJEEVERAM, IN SOUTHERN INDIA, BUT HE GAVE IT ALL *UP* TO FOLLOW THE PATH OF THE ENLIGHTENED ONE!

SOME WHISPERED HE WAS SO SINGLE-MINDED THAT HE HAD *WALKED* ALL THE WAY FROM INDIA!

HE WAS GIVEN A GRAND WELCOME BY *EMPEROR WU* HIMSELF! "I HAVE BUILT MANY TEMPLES AND MONASTERIES," THE EMPEROR SAID. "I HAVE COPIED THE *SACRED BOOKS* OF THE BUDDHA. NOW *WHAT* IS MY MERIT?"

AND THIS *UPPITY FOREIGNER* HAD THE TEMERITY TO REPLY:

"NONE *WHATSOEVER,* YOUR MAJESTY!"

SUCH *HERESY* COULD NOT BE ALLOWED INSIDE THE HALLOWED HALLS OF *SHAOLIN TEMPLE!!*

BUT BODHIDHARMA WAS A *PATIENT* MAN.

HE'D WAIT UNTIL THE MONKS *CHANGED THEIR MINDS.*

SLAM!

AND HE WOULD *WAIT...*

AND *WAIT...*

...FOR *NINE LONG YEARS!*

WHOA... HIS GAZE IS SO *INTENSE* IT BORE A *HOLE* IN THE CLIFFSIDE!

MAYBE HE REALLY *DOES* HAVE SOMETHING TO SHOW US!

ONCE ADMITTED INTO *SHAOLIN*, BODHIDHARMA SET ABOUT TEACHING THE MONKS *HIS* BRAND OF BUDDHISM!

BETWEEN YOU AND ME, I'M GLAD HE'S MAKING US DUMP ALL THIS *COPYING SCRIPTURES*! I WAS COMIN' DOWN WITH *CARPEL TUNNEL*!

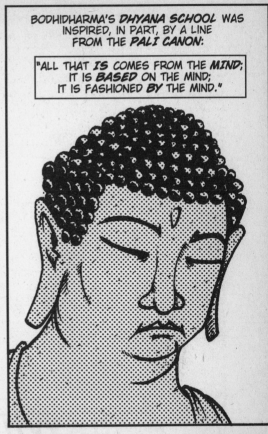

BODHIDHARMA'S *DHYANA SCHOOL* WAS INSPIRED, IN PART, BY A LINE FROM THE *PALI CANON*:

"ALL THAT *IS* COMES FROM THE *MIND*; IT IS *BASED* ON THE MIND; IT IS FASHIONED *BY* THE MIND."

TO BE AT PEACE WITH THE *WORLD*, FIRST YOU HAVE TO BE AT PEACE WITH *YOURSELF*— AND *THAT* IS EASIER SAID THAN *DONE*!

>*PFFFFFT!*< YEAH, RIGHT! *I'M* KEEPIN' IT *REAL*!

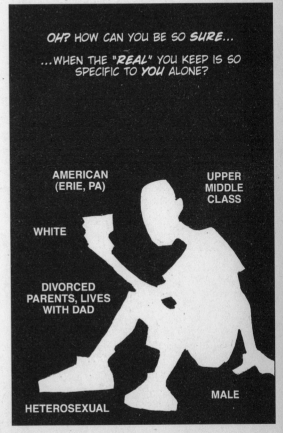

OH? HOW CAN YOU BE SO *SURE*...

...WHEN THE "*REAL*" YOU KEEP IS SO SPECIFIC TO *YOU* ALONE?

AMERICAN (ERIE, PA)

UPPER MIDDLE CLASS

WHITE

DIVORCED PARENTS, LIVES WITH DAD

MALE

HETEROSEXUAL

YOU *PERCEIVE* WHAT IS *REAL* ONLY AS IT IS STRAINED THROUGH YOUR *CONSCIOUSNESS...*

...BUT YOUR CONSCIOUSNESS IS *BIASED* TOWARD YOUR OWN SENSE OF *IDENTITY*, OR *SELF!*

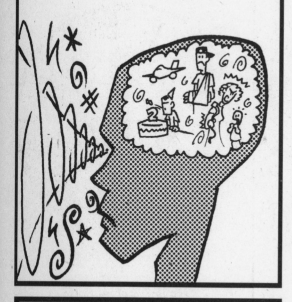

IN *BUDDHISM*, ONLY *ENLIGHTENMENT* - THE ANNIHILATION OF THE *SELF* - CAN *LIBERATE* A PERSON'S CONSCIOUSNESS TO EXPERIENCE UNMEDIATED, *OBJECTIVE* REALITY.

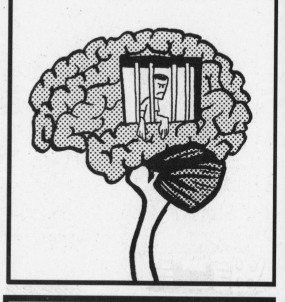

TRADITIONAL BUDDHISM HELD THAT ENLIGHTENMENT WAS A *LIFELONG* PROCESS REQUIRING AN INTENSE *STUDY* OF THE BUDDHA'S TEACHING.

GEEZ, THIS IS TAKING *FOREVER...*

DHARMA

BODHIDHARMA DIDN'T *BUY* THAT. AFTER *ALL...*

THE *BUDDHA* DID NOT HAVE THE SCRIPTURES, YET *HE* BECAME ENLIGHTENED. WHAT DO THE *REST* OF US NEED IT FOR?

HIS *DHAYNA* SCHOOL HELD THAT ENLIGHTENMENT COULD ONLY COME IN THE FORM OF AN *INSTANTANEOUS INSIGHT!*

BODHIDHARMA BELIEVED THAT MAINSTREAM BUDDHISTS USED THE BUDDHA'S LESSONS AS A *CRUTCH* THAT ACTUALLY *HINDERED* ENLIGHTMENT.

HENCE ONE OF HIS MOST FAMOUS *SAYINGS:*

"IF YOU SEE BUDDHA ON THE ROAD...*KILL HIM!*"

MASTER, PLEASE PACIFY MY *MIND!*

SHOW ME THIS MIND, SO THAT I MAY PACIFY IT.

HUH? BUT I *CAN'T* SHOW YOU MY *MIND!*

WELL, THEN...

19

THESE RIDDLES, CALLED **"KOANS,"** DEMONSTRATE THE **ABSURDITY** OF TRUTH, AT LEAST INASMUCH AS IT IS UNDERSTOOD BY THE SUBJECTIVE SELF:

THE POINT ISN'T TO **ANSWER** KOANS, BUT TO CONTEMPLATE WHY THEY **CAN'T** BE ANSWERED!

WORDS AND LANGUAGE ARE ALL COMMUNICATIONS BETWEEN ONE SELF TO ANOTHER, AND THEREFORE USELESS.

IN OTHER WORDS, "FACTS" AS WE KNOW THEM ARE ILLUSIONS! ALL STATEMENTS ARE LANGUAGE, AND BY DEFINITION OPINIONS!

REAL TRUTH IS EXPERIENTIAL, AND CANNOT BE MEDIATED.

IT'S THE ULTIMATE "YOU HAD TO BE THERE."

LANGUAGE... SCIENCE... EVEN ART IS SUBJECTIVE AND CAN'T BE TRUSTED!

THAT *INCLUDES* THIS COMIC STRIP!!

SORRY.

THE ONLY *TRUTH* CONVEYED BY A LANGUAGE-BASED KOAN IS THE LINGERING *QUESTION MARK* WHERE THE ANSWER WOULD BE... *IF ONE EXISTED!*

CONTEMPLATING THIS IN MEDITATION ALLOWS YOU TO *"ENTER THE SILENCE"*...

...WHEREIN THE *DISTINCTIONS* BETWEEN YOU AND THE REST OF THE WORLD OF WHICH YOU ARE A *PART* BREAK DOWN...

...AND YOU ACHIEVE THE *PEACE* ONLY POSSIBLE BY BECOMING *ONE* WITH OBJECTIVE *REALITY.*

THIS WAS HOW BODHIDHARMA PREACHED *DHYANA*, WHICH THE CHINESE MISPRONOUNCED *"CHEN"*...

...AND THE JAPANESE APPROPRIATED AS *"ZEN."*

LONG-TERM MEDITATION IS AS STRENUOUS *PHYSICALLY* AS IT IS MENTALLY. TO KEEP THE SHAOLIN MONKS IN *PEAK* CONDITION, BODHIDHARMA DEVELOPED STRENUOUS *EXERCISES.*

HIS CHARGES RIGHTLY CALLED THESE "HARD WORK..."

...OR, IN CHINESE, *"KUNG FU!"*

NOBODY KNOWS IF BODHIDHARMA ACTUALLY *INTENDED* FOR HIS EXERCISES TO BE DEVELOPED INTO A *PERSONAL DEFENSE SYSTEM...*

...BUT THE LEGENDARY ABILITY OF THE MARTIAL ARTS MASTER TO SIMPLY *REACT* AND *DEFLECT* BLOWS AS THEY'RE AIMED AT HIM IS A *PERFECT* EXAMPLE OF THE ZEN IDEAL OF *ANNIHILATING* THE DISTINCTIONS BETWEEN YOURSELF AND THE REST OF THE WORLD!

MEET ACTION PHILOSOPHER #3:

FRIEDRICH NIETZSCHE!!

COLLECT 'EM ALL!

WRITTEN BY FRED VAN LENTE • ILLUSTRATED BY RYAN DUNLAVEY

NIETZSCHE'S POOR HEALTH FORCES HIM TO PREMATURELY *RETIRE* FROM TEACHING IN 1878, AND NOW HE HAS TIME TO *DEVELOP* HIS ANTI-SOCIALIST IDEAS MORE *THOROUGHLY*... AND HE ENDS UP CRITIQUING *ALL* OF WESTERN SOCIETY!

SAID CRITIQUE CAN PERHAPS BE MOST EASILY SUMMED-UP WITH THE STATEMENT:

"EQUALITY IS A HUMAN-CREATED CONCEPT, *BOGUS* AND ULTIMATELY *CORRUPTING."*

IT'S TOTALLY *ANTITHETICAL* TO OUR *DEMOCRATIC* WAY OF THINKING, BUT *ANOTHER* WAY TO PUT IT IS TO INVOKE THE OLD *PUNK ROCK ETHOS:*

98% OF EVERYTHING IS SHITE!! YEEEEEEAH!!

The ZaraThustras

ALAS, THIS *ALSO* APPLIES TO *PEOPLE.*

FOR EXAMPLE, WHEN WE SEE A *BIG FISH* GET READY TO SWALLOW A *LITTLE FISH*, WE SAY:

AHHHH, THERE'S SUCH *BALANCE* IN *NATURE!*

ONLY THE *FITTEST* CAN *SURVIVE!* IT'S SO *BEAUTIFUL* AND *WISE!*

BUT WHEN A *BIG PERSON* DOES MORE OR LESS THE SAME THING TO A *LITTLE PERSON*, WE SAY:

YOU'RE *EVIL* AND *IMMORAL*--NOT TO MENTION *ARROGANT!*

YOU SHOULD BE THROWN INTO *PRISON* AS A *CRIMINAL!*

Football

WHAT BIG MAN DO? *WHAT BIG MAN DO?!*

EQUALITY IS PHONY AND UNNATURAL BECAUSE, JUST LIKE FISH, SOME PEOPLE ARE BIGGER, STRONGER AND SMARTER THAN OTHERS--BUT ARE PERSECUTED FOR ACTING LIKE IT!

AND, UNIVERSAL EXPERIENCE TELLS US THAT *SOME* PEOPLE ACT LIKE *BIG FISH* ALL THE *TIME*--SO LONG AS THEY HAVE *OTHER* HUMAN-CREATED CONCEPTS LIKE WEALTH, LEGAL OR RELIGIOUS AUTHORITY BACKING THEM *UP*.

EQUALITY IS THEREFORE ALSO *CORRUPTING* BECAUSE IT MAKES ALL OF US *HYPOCRITES*...

...FOR FOLLOWING SOMETHING WE *KNOW* (UNCONSCIOUSLY OR NOT) TO BE A *LIE.*

HOW DID THIS WOEFUL STATE OF AFFAIRS COME **ABOUT?**

ONCE UPON A TIME, TENS OF **THOUSANDS** OF YEARS AGO, THE SMARTEST AND **STRONGEST** OF ANY GIVEN GROUP OF HUMANS **NATURALLY** BECAME THEIR **RULER**--

UNCA' FRIEDRICH'S Bedtime Stories

"-I CALL THIS PERSON AN **ÜBERMENSCH**, OR **'SUPERMAN.'**"

I'M **TIRED** OF THE SUPERMAN GETTING ALL THAT **TAIL!**

THE SUPERMAN KICKED MY **ASS** FOR NOT WORKING THE **MAMMOTH PITS!** I TRIED TO FIGHT BACK, BUT HE'S SO MUCH **STRONGER** THAN ME!

ME MUST THINK OF...DUH...**SUMPIN'** TO **GET** DAT SOOPERMAN!

"SO THE **JEALOUS MASSES** BANDED **TOGETHER** AND **INVENTED**..."

>WHISPER< >WHISPER< >MUMBLE<
>MUMBLE< >MUTTER< >RHUBARB<
>MUTTER<

...**RELIGION!!**

I AM GOD!! I AM AN INVISIBLE, SUPERNATURAL ENTITY THAT IS GREATER THAN THE SUPERMAN!!

YOU MUST **OBEY ME, NOT HIM!!** AND BECAUSE I AM INVISIBLE, ALL MY COMMANDS MUST BE DICTATED BY...

...THE **PRIEST RACE,** HERE!

THERE **IS NO** SUPERMAN!

ALL ARE EQUAL IN THE EYES OF GOD!

ANYONE CAN BE A **SUPERMAN!**

WELL GOH-LLEE!

"EVER **SINCE**, WESTERN SOCIETY HAS RETAINED THIS **BASIC** MONOTHEISTIC IDEAL..."

EVERYONE IS EQUAL IN THE **FREE MARKETS!**

ALL ARE EQUAL IN THE EYES OF THE **LAW!**

"BUT THE MASTER **'PRIEST'** CLASS ALWAYS MAKES SURE **IT'S** MORE EQUAL THAN **OTHERS!**"

"ALAS, SINCE EQUALITY IS **BOGUS**, THIS **'OPIUM OF THE MASSES'** IS ULTIMATELY **UNSATISFYING**, SINCE **LITTLE** FISH CAN'T SUDDENLY **TRANSFORM** INTO **BIG** FISH BY A PROCESS OF **SELF-DETERMINATION!**"

"YOU **MIGHT** AS WELL GET MISERABLE AND DEPRESSED BECAUSE..."

WAAAH!! I WANNA SPROUT **WINGS** AND FLY TO **VENUS!**

"WITHOUT THE **NATURAL** LEADERSHIP OF THE SUPERMAN, THE ALWAYS-**DISAPPOINTED** MASSES AND THE **MASTER RACE** ARE LOCKED IN A PERPETUAL-BUT-**MEANINGLESS** STRUGGLE FOR **TEMPORAL POWER.**"

"MARTIN LUTHER'S **PROTESTANT REFORMATION**-THE MUTATION OF **FUEDALISM** INTO **CAPITALISM**--THE **AMERICAN** AND **FRENCH** REVO-LUTIONS--**NONE** OF THEM HAVE CHANGED A **THING**...AND **COMMUNISM** WON'T BE ANY **DIFFERENT!**"

"**NONE** OF THESE 'REVOLUTIONS' ADDRESS THE **REAL** SOURCE OF THE MASSES' DESPAIR."

"THE INVENTION OF GOD MADE THE SUPERMAN STOP BELIEVING IN HIS **OWN** EXISTENCE!"

MY WIFE'S GONNA **KILL** ME IF I DON'T GET THAT **BONUS!**

WHY DON'T MORE PEOPLE **LIKE** ME?

THIS **PIMPLE** ON MY **ASS** REALLY HURTS!

BUT UNCA **FRIEDRICH**, HOW CAN HUMAN MISERY BE **RELIEVED?**

BEATS THE HECK OUTTA **ME**, KID.

GENERALLY SPEAKING, NIETZSCHE WAS A **NIHILIST** AND A **PESSIMIST** WHO BELIEVED THAT LIFE **WAS** MISERY.

STILL, ALL THE *SCIENTIFIC DISCOVERIES* OF THE 19TH CENTURY *SHOOK* BELIEF IN ORGANIZED RELIGION, LEADING HIM TO FAMOUSLY PROCLAIM IN *'THUS SPAKE ZARATHUSTRA'* (1885) THAT:

GOD IS *DEAD!*

I DIDN'T DO IT.

AND *THAT* MEANT:

I REMEMBER WHO I AM!!

THE *SUPERMAN!!* YOU'RE *BACK!!* YAAAAAY!!

BUT WHO *WAS* THE SUPERMAN? NIETZSCHE *FIRST* LATCHED ONTO ULTRANATIONALIST COMPOSER *RICHARD WAGNER*, HE OF *RING OF THE NIBELUNG* FAME.

NIETZSCHE BECAME WAGNER'S BIGGEST *CHEERLEADER* IN THE EARLY 1870'S, HELPING HIM RAISE *FUNDS* AND LIONIZING HIM IN *PRINT*.

LIKE GREECE'S *AESCHYLUS*, THE MAJESTY OF HIS *OPERA* WILL PACIFY AND *UNIFY* THE GERMAN MASSES AND MAKE THEM *FORGET* COMMUNISM! >SIGH!<

BUT WHEN WAGNER BECOMES A *BORN-AGAIN CHRISTIAN* NIETZSCHE ABANDONS HIM AND THE CONCEPT OF *SALVATION* THROUGH *ART*.

NIETZSCHE *EVEN* GOES SO FAR AS WRITE SCATHING *CONDEMNA-TIONS* OF HIS FORMER FRIEND, CULMINATING IN *'NIETZSCHE CONTRA WAGNER'* (1895).

ALMOST *ALL* OF NIETZSCHE'S MAJOR WORKS OF PHILOSOPHY--*"BEYOND GOOD AND EVIL"*--*"TWILIGHT OF THE IDOLS"*--ARE WRITTEN LESS THAN A DECADE INTO HIS RETIREMENT.

SPX SMALL PHILOSOPHER'S EXPO

KNOW-NOTHING *JERKS!* >GRUMBLE<

KISS MY BUTT ONLY $50!

50% OFF!

BUT *FEW* OF HIS *SELF-PUBLISHED* BOOKS SELL MORE THAN 100 *COPIES*, AND NIETZSCHE REMAINS *UNKNOWN* BEYOND A VERY *SMALL* CADRE OF ADMIRERS. (MANY OF THEM *EUROPEAN NOBILITY*).

HIS HEALTH--PHYSICAL *AND* MENTAL--DETERIORATES DUE TO PROSTITUTE-CONTRACTED SYPHILIS AND HE HAS TO MOVE BACK IN WITH HIS *MOM* IN 1889.

THOUGH HE BECAME CONVINCED *GUESS-WHO* WAS *YOU-KNOW-WHAT*, HE DIED MOSTLY IGNORED BY THE INTELLECTUAL COMMUNITY IN 1900.

IN JUNE, 1776, THE **CONTINENTAL CONGRESS** OF THE REBELLIOUS THIRTEEN AMERICAN COLONIES COULD AGREE ON ALMOST **NOTHING** -- EXCEPT THE NEED TO **ARTICULATE** THEIR GRIEVANCES WITH THE **BRITISH CROWN!**

THE MAN DRAFTED TO **DRAFT** THIS **DECLARATION** WAS THE **QUIETEST** DELEGATE IN CONGRESS--A MAN WHOSE OWN **SPEAKING VOICE** BARELY ROSE ABOVE A **WHISPER**--BUT WAS **UNANIMOUSLY AGREED** TO BE THE GREATEST **POLITICAL WRITER** IN THE COUNTRY...

...A MAN **WE** KNOW BETTER AS **ACTION PHILOSOPHER #4:**

Thomas Jefferson!

We mutually pledge to each other our lives, our fortunes and our sacred honor:
Frederick J. Van Lente (script)
Ryan Michael Dunlavey (art)

JEFFERSON AUTHORED WHAT TURNED OUT TO BE **AMERICAN SCRIPTURE**, BUT IT WAS THE **CROWNING ACHIEVEMENT** OF **THE ENLIGHTENMENT**, ITSELF A **REVOLUTIONARY** SHIFT IN EUROPEAN PHILOSOPHY!

IN CONGRESS. JULY 4, 1776.

The unanimous Declaration of the .... States of America.

UNLESS, OF COURSE, YOU PREFER THE *"GOD IS A TOTAL RETARD"* THEORY.

MANY CRITICS DERIDED THE ENLIGHTENMENT THINKERS AS HOPELESSLY *NAIVE.* AFTER ALL, THIS WAS A *RADICAL DEVIATION* FROM *CENTURIES* OF CHRISTIAN THOUGHT!

THROUGHOUT THE *MIDDLE AGES* IT WAS PRESUMED THAT HUMANS WERE HOPE-LESSLY *CORRUPT.* OUR EXPULSION FROM EDEN *ALIENATED* US FROM GOD AND WE WOULD ACHIEVE UNION WITH HIM ONLY IN *DEATH!*

TO ENLIGHTENMENT THINKERS, HOWEVER, THIS ALIENATION WAS THE RESULT OF AN OVERLY COMPLICATED, *MANMADE* ECCLESIASTICAL BUREAUCRACY THAT HAD NO *COUNTERPART* IN NATURE!

I'M *SORRY,* SIR, HE'S *VERY* BUSY, SO IF YOU DON'T HAVE AN *APPOINTMENT* I'M AFRAID I CAN'T LET YOU IN...

GOD

Z

ONLY BY DOING *AWAY* WITH MANMADE *CONSTRUCTS* AND CLEAVING CLOSE TO OUR *OWN* INNATE *NATURE* COULD WE BE TRULY GOOD, INNOCENT, AND (THEREFORE) CLOSER TO *GOD...*

Zip!

...A SO-CALLED *"NOBLE SAVAGE!"*

AH-AAAAAHHH!-

THOMAS JEFFERSON WAS THE NOBLE SAVAGE *INCARNATE!* HE WAS BORN IN *1743* ON THE *EDGE* OF SETTLED VIRGINIA!

HIS UPWARDLY MOBILE FATHER *INSISTED* ON GIVING HIM A *CLASSICAL EDUCATION* WITH AN EMPHASIS ON *ENLIGHTENMENT PHILOSOPHY.*

FROM HIS ISOLATED RURAL *PLANTATION,* MONTICELLO -- THE HOUSE HE *DESIGNED* FOR HIMSELF -- JEFFERSON FOUND TIME TO --

Vote
☐ Yeh
☑ Nay

SERVE IN THE VIRGINIA *LEGISLATURE*

MAINTAIN A *LEGAL* PRACTICE

INVENT A *LAP DESK* AND AN IMPROVED *PLOW*

BECOME AN ACCOMPLISHED *VIOLINIST*

AND AMASS OVER 6,400 *BOOKS,* WHICH WOULD SERVE AS THE *BASIS* FOR THE *U.S. LIBRARY OF CONGRESS!*

JEFFERSON'S ENTIRE *LEGISLATIVE CAREER* INVOLVED FREEING THE COLONY'S CITIZENS TO FIND THEIR *OWN* INNER NOBLE SAVAGE!

HE *WROTE* THE STATUTE GUARANTEEING VIRGINIANS' *RELIGIOUS FREEDOM* TO FIND GOD IN *THEIR OWN* WAY!

GOD
(NO MENUS)

WORLD'S GREATEST EVERYTHING

→SNORT!←
HUH? WHA..?

I'M *SO GLAD* THE *MEDIEVAL EUROPEAN* SYSTEM OF *PRIMOGENITURE* MAINTAINS AN *AMERICAN* ARISTOCRACY BY FORCING *ALL LANDS* TO BE INHERITED BY THE *ELDEST SON* -GAK!!

BELIEVING THIS SYSTEM *UNNATURAL* TOO, JEFFERSON SPEARHEADED *ENDING* IT, SO *ALL* WOULD HAVE THE OPPORTUNITY TO *WORK THE LAND!*

YOU CAN ONLY *IMAGINE* HOW HE FELT ABOUT THE *BRITISH* ARISTOCRACY, WHICH *RULED* AMERICA FROM *LONDON!*

HE WAS ONE OF THE *FIRST* REVOLUTIONARIES TO OPENLY ADVOCATE *FULL* SUCCESSION FROM ENGLAND, IN 1774!

FOR THE DECLARATION OF INDEPENDENCE JEFFERSON TURNED IN SOME OF THE CATCHIEST *AD SLOGANS* FOR *DEMOCRACY* IN *HISTORY!*

BUT HE WAS NO *HIPPIE.* "PURSUIT OF HAPPINESS" HAD A VERY *SPECIFIC* MEANING TO SOMEONE OF HIS *CLASS*...

LIFE, LIBERTY and the PURSUIT of HAPPINESS

...IN JEFFERSON'S MIND AMERICA WAS TO BECOME AN *AGRARIAN PARADISE* DOMINATED BY *FARMER/INTELLECTUALS!*

THEM *V.R. GOGGLES* RUNNIN' ON TH' *COLD FUSION REACTOR* THAR, PA?

YESSUM. INVENTED THE GOL-DANGED THING AFTER I MILKED THE *HOG*, I DID.

POTATOES

YOU MEND THE *CHICKEN COOP* AND FINISH THAT MONOGRAPH ON THE NATURAL RIGHTS OF *PROPERTY* YET?

ALL IN ITS OWN GOOD *TIME,* MOTHER ...

IN OTHER WORDS, IF LEFT TO THEIR OWN DEVICES, *ALL* AMERICANS WOULD *NATURALLY* TURN OUT JUST LIKE *JEFFERSON!*

THERE WAS ONLY ONE SLIGHT *PROBLEM* WITH THIS PLAN, HOWEVER.

WHAT ABOUT *US*?

JEFFERSON WASN'T ENTIRELY "JEFFERSON" *HIMSELF*!

HIS "*NATURAL*" EXISTENCE WAS LARGELY A RESULT OF A *MAN-MADE* CONSTRUCT--ONE OF THE MOST *HEINOUS* IN HISTORY!

ABOUT *200 AFRICAN SLAVES* DID ALL OF JEFFERSON'S FARMING FOR HIM, GRANTING HIM THE *LUXURY* TO LIVE A LIFE OF THOUGHT AND SCIENCE!

FREEDOM

HOW TO *RECONCILE* SUCH AN *OBVIOUS* CONTRADICTION BETWEEN *IDEAL* AND *REALITY*?

"ALL MEN ARE CREATED EQUAL"

TAP TAP

EASY...

NOT MEN

HEY! QUIT IT!

"...NEGROES ARE NOT *MEN*!"

BETTER PULL UP A *CHAIR*. SOMETHING TELLS ME YOU'RE GONNA BE *STUCK* HERE UNTIL THE 1960'S.

HA! YOU'RE NOT SO TOUGH *NOW*, ARE YA, MR. "I'VE-GOT-OPPOSABLE-THUMBS!"

"IN *REASON* (BLACKS ARE) MUCH *INFERIOR*... *NEVER* COULD I FIND THAT A BLACK HAD UTTERED A THOUGHT ABOVE THE LEVEL OF PLAIN *NARRATION*."*

PRETTY *SIMPLE*, RIGHT?

*: T.J., *NOTES ON VIRGINIA* (1783)

JEFFERSON'S *REAL* GENIUS LAY NOT JUST IN HIS *IDEAS*--BUT IN HIS ABILITY TO *CONVEY* THEM IN EASY-TO-UNDERSTAND TERMS! HE SAW ALL CONFLICTS AS STARK *WHITE* VERSUS *BLACK*!

(IF YOU'LL PARDON THE TERM.)

THIS *ACCESSIBILITY* OF HIS PHILOSOPHY HAS INSPIRED WOULD-BE *REVOLUTIONARIES* OF *EVERY* STRIPE EVER SINCE!

A T-SHIRT WITH *THIS* QUOTATION WAS FOUND IN THE APARTMENT OF OKLAHOMA CITY BOMBER *TIMOTHY McVEIGH*:

"The tree of liberty must be refreshed from time to time with the blood of patriots and tyrants."

— Thomas Jefferson

HE PROVED MUCH MORE ADROIT AT FIGHTING *BAD* LAWS THAN SUPPORTING *GOOD* ONES.

IRONICALLY, AMERICA'S GREATEST POLITICAL THEORIST *MISSED* THE ENTIRE *CONSTITUTIONAL DEBATES* SERVING AS THE USA'S AMBASSADOR TO FRANCE!

THERE HE DISTURBED MANY OF HIS COMRADES WITH HIS UNEQUIVOCAL SUPPORT OF THE BLOOD-SOAKED *FRENCH REVOLUTION*:

"RATHER THAN IT SHOULD HAVE *FAILED*, I WOULD HAVE SEEN HALF THE *EARTH* DESOLATED!"

BY THE MIDDLE OF HIS FIRST TERM AS *PRESIDENT*, JEFFERSON HAD MADE MANY ENEMIES, WHO THOUGHT HE WAS A *DANGEROUS RADICAL*. IN 1802 THEY SPREAD REPORTS THAT ALLEGED:

PRESIDENT JEFFERSON KEEPS ONE OF HIS *OWN SLAVES* AS HIS *MISTRESS!*

FRIGGIN' *ATTACK ADS...*

IN 1998, *D.N.A. TESTING* ON DESCENDANTS PROVED THAT *SALLY HEMMINGS*, A SLAVE 20 YEARS JEFFERSON'S JUNIOR, WAS HIS *LOVER* FOR *DECADES!*

JEFFERSON'S YOUNG WIFE HAD DIED IN 1781. RIGHT BEFORE THE *END*, SHE MADE HIM *PROMISE*:

YOU MUST *NEVER* ... MARRY ... AGAIN!

AND HE *DIDN'T*.

BUT JEFFERSON WAS *38*--NOT EXACTLY *CHASTE WIDOWER* MATERIAL--AND HE HAD A *POIGNANT* TEMPTATION LIVING RIGHT UNDER HIS *ROOF*:

JEFFERSON *INHERITED* SALLY HEMMINGS AND *99 OTHER* SLAVES FROM HIS WIFE'S *FATHER*. SALLY'S MOTHER *BETTY* WAS JEFFERSON'S *FATHER-IN-LAW*'S MISTRESS...

...SALLY WAS JEFFERSON'S *DEAD WIFE'S HALF-SISTER!*

OH YEAH! *NOW* YOU'RE TALKIN'!

WAS THIS A WAY OF HAVING HIS CAKE AND EATING IT TOO ... DID KEEPING AN ALLEGED *INFERIOR* AS HIS LOVER "NOT COUNT" AS BREAKING HIS PROMISE TO HIS WIFE?

AFTER ALL, THIS *IS* THE SAME MAN WHO TRIED TO BE A *SLAVEHOLDING* GURU OF PERSONAL FREEDOM!

"NOTHING IS MORE CERTAINLY WRITTEN IN THE BOOK OF *FATE*, THAT THESE PEOPLE (BLACKS) ARE MEANT TO BE *FREE*..."

"...NOR IS IT *LESS* CERTAIN THAT THE TWO RACES *CANNOT* LIVE IN THE *SAME* GOVERNMENT!"*

*: T.J., *AUTOBIOGRAPHY* (1821)

DESPITE HIS *RACISM*, JEFFERSON BELIEVED SLAVERY WAS *WRONG*-- YET IT WAS THE ONE *UNNATURAL* CONSTRUCT HE COULD *NOT* SLAY.

HIS ORIGINAL DRAFT OF THE *DECLARATION OF INDEPENDENCE* CONTAINED A PASSAGE *CONDEMNING* SLAVERY, BUT IT WAS EXCISED AT THE DEMAND OF *SOUTHERN DELAGATES!*

WHEN HE WAS A YOUTHFUL MEMBER OF THE VIRGINIA LEGISTLATURE, JEFFERSON INTRODUCED A BILL *ABOLISHING* SLAVERY, BUT IT WAS VOTED DOWN!

PERPETUALLY IN *DEBT* AFTER THE REVOLUTION, HE WOULD HAVE BEEN *RUINED* IF HE FREED HIS *OWN* SLAVES -- WHICH, AS PROPERTY, COULD BE USED FOR *EQUITY!*

-HEH-... SORRY ABOUT THIS GUYS... -GULP!-

HE DEALT WITH HIS FAILURES AND CONTRADICTIONS BY *IGNORING* THEM! SLAVERY ... INFIDELITY ... THESE HAD *NO* PLACE IN HIS BLACK-AND-WHITE WORLD, SO HE *DEFERRED* CONFRONTING THEM *INDEFINITELY!*

LA-LA-LA, I CAN'T *HEAR* YOU...

SLAVERY *BLINDED* HIM TO AMERICA'S *TRUE* DESTINY-- WHICH WAS *INDUSTRIAL* AND *URBAN*, NOT PASTORAL AND AGRARIAN.

!%@#$!

AMERICA'S DEFERRAL OF THE *SLAVERY* ISSUE *EXPLODED* WHEN SLAVEHOLDING STATES TRIED TO *SECEDE* FROM THE UNION...

...QUOTING *JEFFERSON* AS JUSTIFICATION FOR THEIR *REBELLION*, OF COURSE.

AS INSPIRING AS JEFFERSON'S *WORDS* WERE, IT WOULD BE THE *BLOOD* SPILLED DURING THE *CIVIL WAR* THAT WOULD AT LAST REALIZE HIS *VISION* OF EQUALITY FOR *ALL.*

DOES **THIS MAN** LOOK LIKE A *SAINT* TO YOU?!

HE SURE LOOKS LIKE ACTION PHILOSOPHER #5:

St. Augustine!

WRITTEN (THANKS TO *GRACE*) BY FRED VAN LENTE!

DRAWN (OF HIS OWN FREE *WILL*) BY RYAN DUNLAVEY!

BORN IN *A.D. 354* IN WHAT IS NOW SOUIK-AHRAS, ALGERIA, AURELIUS AUGUSTINE WAS RAISED A *CHRISTIAN* BY HIS DEVOUT MOTHER, *MONICA*. BUT HER FAITH DIDN'T STICK--AT *FIRST*. FOR *ONE* THING, HIS RAGING HORMONES WEREN'T INTERESTED...

"GIVE ME *CHASTITY* AND *CONTINENCE*...

"...JUST NOT *NOW!*"* (CHOMINA, HOMINA!)

*: ST. A., *CONFESSIONS* (A.D. 400)

41

...AND NEITHER WAS HIS *RAGING INTELLECT!*

CHRISTIANITY CONTAINS TOO MANY *CONTRADICTIONS.* MOTHER SAYS THAT GOD IS NOT ONLY *GOOD* BUT GOODNESS *ITSELF...*

...BUT HOW COULD THIS *SAME* GOD ALSO CREATE THE *WICKED WILL* THAT ALLOWS PEOPLE TO DO *EVIL?* WOULDN'T HE WANT *EVERYONE* TO BE GOOD--AND THEN JUST *MAKE* THEM THAT WAY FROM BIRTH?

CHRISTIANS *THEMSELVES* CAN'T EVEN AGREE ON THE MOST *BASIC TENTS* OF THEIR OWN RELIGION!

ONLY A FEW CENTURIES OLD, CHRISTIANITY WAS STILL IN A *MOLTEN* STATE. ITS FORMAL *DOGMA* HAD YET TO *SOLIDIFY,* AND PROLIFERATING SECTS WERE *LEGION.*

HEED THE WISDOM OF *NESTORIANISM,* INFIDELS! CHRIST IS *TWO ENTITIES,* ONE DIVINE, THE OTHER *HUMAN!*

UM, WE *MONOTHELITES* WOULD LIKE TO HUMBLY ASSERT THAT CHRIST HAS *ONE WILL* BUT *TWO NATURES,* BUT, UH, HE *CLEAVES* TOWARD THE *DIVINE.*

YOU *DARE* PROMOTE YOUR *DONATISM* OVER MY *ARIANISM?* WE TEACH THAT GOD THE *FATHER* IS THE *ONLY* TRUE GOD--JESUS AND THE HOLY SPIRIT ARE MERELY HIS *CREATIONS!*

WE *ADOPTIONISTS* WOULD HAVE YOU *BURNT AT THE STAKE* FOR SUCH *BLASPHEMY!* CHRIST WAS A *MAN,* IMBUED WITH THE *SPIRIT* OF GOD!

FALSE PROPHET! CHRIST HAS *ONE NATURE* --DIVINE! *ALL* ADHERENTS TO *MONOPHYSITISM* KNOW THIS!

WHATEVER *THAT* MEANS! ->PFFFFT!<- CALL ME WHEN YOU GET YOUR *STORIES STRAIGHT...* LOSERS!

INSTEAD, AUGUSTINE DRIFTED TOWARD PAGAN *MANICHAEISM.*

FRIENDS, HOW CAN *GOOD* EXIST WITHOUT *EVIL?* HOW COULD WE SEE THE *LIGHT* IF IT DID NOT PIERCE THE *DARK?* AND IS IT NOT *SUNSHINE* THAT CAUSES *SHADOWS* TO FALL?

THE TEACHINGS OF GREAT *MANI* REVEAL THIS AND MUCH, MUCH *MORE!*

THE IRAQI MYSTIC *MANI*, A.K.A. "THE *ILLUSTRIOUS ONE*," SYNTHESIZED VARIOUS KIBBLES & BITS OF BUDDHISM, BABYLONIAN MYTHOLOGY AND ZOROASTRIAN *DUALISM* INTO A PHILOSOPHY THAT SPREAD LIKE *WILDFIRE* THROUGHOUT EUROPE, ASIA AND THE MIDDLE EAST IN THE *THIRD CENTURY*.

MANI TAUGHT THAT IN THE BEGINNING THE UNIVERSE WAS DIVIDED INTO A REALM OF *LIGHT* AND A REALM OF *DARKNESS*. EACH WAS INFINITE IN *ALL* DIRECTIONS SAVE *ONE*, WHICH WAS WHERE THE TWO REALMS *MET*.

HEE HEE HEE

1 FINITE POINT IN **UNIVERSE** GIFT SHOP

RESTROOM FOR CUSTOMERS ONLY!

HE BECAME *SO* POPULAR THAT THE *PERSIAN EMPIRE* OUTLAWED THE SECT AND IMPRISONED ITS FOUNDER. THOUGH MANI DIED IN *CHAINS* IN 277, MANICHAEISM CONTINUED TO FLOURISH AS ONE OF CHRISTIANITY'S *BIGGEST COMPETITORS*.

ALL MIGHT HAVE REMAINED PEACEFUL IN THIS *"DUOVERSE"* FOREVER, EXCEPT...

MY DARK DOMAIN WOULD BE PERFECT NIGHT WERE IT NOT FOR THE GALLING GLOW SEEPING IN FROM THE ACCURSED KINGDOM OF LIGHT!

THOOM! THOOM! THOOM!

HARK! THE FEARSOME FOOTFALLS OF THE DARKNESS KING DOTH APPROACH!

THOOM! THOOM! THOOM!

VERILY, A HERO MUST RISE AND VANQUISH THE MASTER OF MALFEASANCE BEFORE HE SPOILS MINE LUMINESCENT LAND!

44

AND SO THE **SONS** OF FIRSTMAN DID BATTLE WITH THEIR DIAMETRIC **OPPOSITES** AMONG THE BROOD OF THE KING OF **DARKNESS**.

CLEAR AIR!

PESTILENT BREATH!

REFRESHING WIND!

SCORCHING WIND!

BRIGHT LIGHT!

GLOOM!

MIST!

LIFE-GIVING WATERS!

WARMING FIRE!

CONSUMING FIRE!

THE SONS OF LIGHT **WON,** AND THE VANQUISHED CORPSES OF THE SONS OF **DARKNESS** BECAME THE MATTER THAT FORMED THE HEAVENS AND THE **EARTH.**

FINITE POINT! UNIVERSE GIFT SHOP

SINCE **HUMANS** CAME OUT OF THAT **MATTER,** WE'RE MADE OUT OF THE **STUFF** OF DARKNESS--EVIL!

MANI SAYS THAT PICKING FIGS TO EAT IS TANTAMOUNT TO *SLAYING* THEM AND THEREFORE *EVIL*. SO, TO STAY *PURE*, THE ELECT MUST HAVE THEIR FOOD PICKED *FOR* THEM.

BUT SIMPLE *LOGIC* DICTATES THAT FORCING *OTHERS* TO DO EVIL ON YOUR BEHALF IS ITSELF *EVIL*!

LOOK, YOU SEEM LIKE A *BRIGHT KID*, SO I'M NOT GONNA B.S. YOU: I *CAN'T* EXPLAIN THAT DISCREPANCY...

...BUT SINCE MOST PEOPLE ARE TOO *STUPID* TO UNDERSTAND *HALF* THE STUFF YOU TALK ABOUT, WHO *CARES*? KEEP IT *SIMPLE*: STICK WITH THE GOOD-VERSUS-EVIL STUFF, AND PEOPLE DIE HAPPY ... AND *UNCONFUSED*. YA DIG?

AUGUSTINE WAS SO *DEMORALIZED* BY HIS ENCOUNTER WITH FAUSTUS THAT HE *GAVE UP* BEING A MANICHEAN... IN FACT, HE NEARLY GAVE UP ON *RELIGION* ALTOGETHER!

IN A.D. 383, AUGUSTINE MOVED TO *ITALY* AND BECAME A MUCH SOUGHT-AFTER TEACHER OF *RHETORIC*, INSTRUCTING THE YOUNG *HELLIONS* OF ROMAN ARISTOCRACY HOW TO *TWIST* THE TRUTH TO THEIR ADVANTAGE THROUGH A CUNNING USE OF *LANGUAGE*.

LESSON 1:
HOW TO LIE

AS SKILLED AS HE *WAS*, IT WAS STILL A *STRUGGLE*. IT WAS QUITE COMMON IN THOSE DAYS FOR STUDENTS TO *DROP* A CLASS RIGHT BEFORE *TUITION* WAS DUE--

--AND CONTINUE THEIR COURSEWORK WITH *ANOTHER* INSTRUCTOR ACROSS TOWN!

"*GOOD* IS JUST ANOTHER WAY OF SAYING 'WHAT *GOD* WANTS US TO DO.'"

"BUT ONLY IN *EDEN* WAS MAN'S *FREE WILL* PERFECTLY *IN SYNCH* WITH HIS CREATOR'S-- ADAM'S *WANTS* WERE THE SAME AS GOD'S!"

"AFTER OUR EXPULSION FROM THE GARDEN, WE BECAME *SEPARATED* FROM THE LORD. SINCE EVIL IS, IN ESSENCE, THE *ABSENCE* OF GOD, AFTER OUR *FALL FROM GRACE* IT BECAME THE MOST *COMMON* THING ON EARTH!"

"TODAY, ADAM'S *SONS AND DAUGHTERS* ARE LOST IN *MORAL CONFUSION.* WE NO LONGER *INSTINCTUALLY* KNOW THE *GOOD.*"

25¢

PLEASE HELP
GOD BLESS

"IN FACT, WE *CANNOT DO GOOD* WITHOUT AN *INVITATION FROM GOD*-- HIS *GRACE*, WHICH HE SENDS TO US BECAUSE HE *WANTS* US TO BE SAVED!"

PLEASE HELP
GOD BLESS

"THOUGH HUMAN WILL IS *CAPABLE* OF RESISTING GOD'S GRACE, NO ONE EVER *DOES.* GRACE IS TOO ENTICING TO *IGNORE*, FOR IT REMINDS US OF OUR ORIGINAL HOME, *EDEN!*"

BUT IF HUMANITY CANNOT *RESIST* GRACE, AND IT IS *GOD* WHO CHOOSES *WHO* TO GIVE GRACE *TO*, IT IS THE *LORD* WHO DECIDES WHO IS SAVED, *NOT* INDIVIDUAL HUMANS. HOW CAN *THAT* BE CALLED *FREE WILL?*

WITH ALL DUE RESPECT, MOTHER, YOU FAIL TO TAKE INTO ACCOUNT AN OBVIOUS POINT:

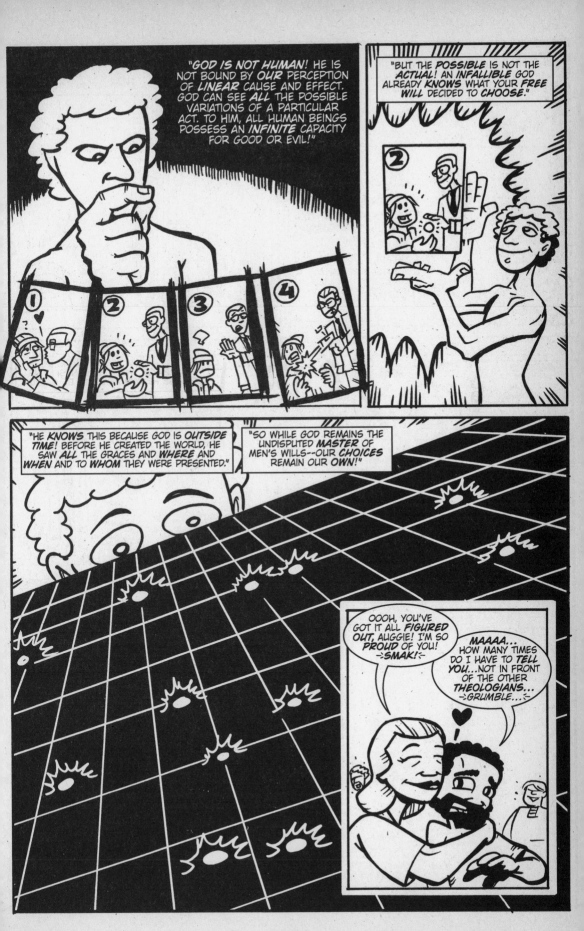

THE BISHOP OF MILAN, *ST. AMBROSE*, BAPTIZED AUGUSTINE ON *EASTER*, 387.

HE SOLD *ALL* HIS WORLDLY POSSESSIONS AND PLANNED TO LEAD A LIFE OF *PRAYER* AND *THOUGHT*...BUT FATE HAD *OTHER* PLANS.

AUGUSTINE'S MOTHER DIED MERE *MONTHS* AFTER HIS BAPTISM. PERHAPS NOT COINCIDENTALLY, SOON THEREAFTER HE RETURNED TO *MOTHER AFRICA*... SPECIFICALLY *HIPPO*, A CITY IN WHAT IS NOW *TUNISIA*.

MONICA WOULD LATER BE *CANONIZED* ALONG WITH HER SON AS THE PATRON SAINT OF *ABUSED WIVES* (AUGGIE'S DAD WAS A *PAGAN*).

ALREADY *FAMOUS* FOR THE WRITINGS THAT HE HAD PRODUCED DURING HIS *SOLITUDE* OUTSIDE MILAN, AUGUSTINE WAS PERSUADED BY THE LOCAL FAITHFUL TO BE *ORDAINED* INTO THE PRIESTHOOD.

IN 396 HE WAS ELECTED *BISHOP OF HIPPO*, THE MOST IMPORTANT SEE IN AFRICA, AN OFFICE HE WOULD HOLD FOR THE NEXT THIRTY-FOUR YEARS!

BISHOP AUGUSTINE SPECIALIZED IN THE ERADICATION OF *HERESY* THROUGH *REASON*. HIS *ORATORICAL SKILLS* QUICKLY BECAME *LEGENDARY*.

AT THE CLIMAX OF HIS DEBATE WITH THE MANICHEAN *FELIX* IN 404, THE ELECT WAS SO *PERSUADED* BY THE BISHOP'S WORDS THAT HE *CONVERTED* ON THE *SPOT*!

HIS SYSTEM OF *DIVINE GRACE* PUT THE KIBOSH ON THE *PELAGIAN* HERESIES, WHICH *DENIED* THE EXISTENCE OF *ORIGINAL SIN*!

THE WINNNNNNNNNAH-- *AUGUSTINE!*

THANKS TO AUGUSTINE'S REASONED EXPLICATION OF THEOLOGY AND DOGMA, THE VARIOUS COMPETING SECTS FELL INTO DISREPAIR, AND THE CHURCH OF ROME THAT THE BISHOP OF HIPPO REPRESENTED--WHICH BECAME KNOWN AS THE *"CATHOLIC"*, OR *"UNIVERSAL"* CHURCH, GREW EVER STRONGER!

AUGUSTINE BATTLED HERESY *LITERALLY* TO HIS DYING DAYS. WHILE HE PASSED AWAY IN 430, THE *VANDALS*, ADHERENTS OF *ARIANISM* (SEE PG. 42), WERE *LAYING SIEGE* TO HIPPO!

ONE OF THE MOST *PROLIFIC* THINKERS EVER, AUGUSTINE REFUTED COMPETING SECTS LIKE THE *DONATISTS* (WHICH HELD THAT ONLY THE *MORALLY PURE* COULD BECOME *PRIESTS*) WITH OVER *ONE THOUSAND SEPARATE WORKS* ON CHRISTIAN THOUGHT AND CHURCH DOCTRINE!

OHHHH...!!

AFTER HIS CANONIZATION, HE BECAME THE PATRON SAINT OF *BREWERS* (FOR HIS FORMERLY WILD WAYS) AND, OF COURSE, *THEOLOGIANS...*

...BUT *MOST IMPORTANTLY*, HE IS KNOWN AS THE *GREATEST* OF THE CHURCH *FATHERS.* HIS *FEAST DAY* IS *AUGUST 28TH.*

NOW MARY, CAN YOU *EXPLAIN* WHAT WE *LEARNED* TODAY?

UH...WE DO *GOOD THINGS* BECAUSE GOD *PERSUADES* US WITH GRACE, EVEN THOUGH WE'RE NOT CONSCIOUSLY *AWARE* OF IT?

RIGHT.

EXCEPT...GOD *GAVE* US THE GRACE IN THE FIRST PLACE BECAUSE HE *KNEW* BEFOREHAND WE WOULD *PAY ATTENTION* TO IT.

EXACTLY!

THAT'S BECAUSE... OF ALL INFINITE POSSIBLE UNIVERSES, *THIS ONE* IS WHAT GOD, USING *HIS* FREE WILL, *CHOSE* TO CREATE, WITH *THESE* OUTCOMES.

YES, YES! WELL *DONE!*

BUT...WHY IF *GOD* HAS FREE WILL, THEN WHY DID HE CHOOSE *THIS* UNIVERSE, AND NOT ONE OF THE *OTHER* POSSIBLE UNIVERSES WHERE *GOOD* PEOPLE DIDN'T GET GRACE AND *BAD* PEOPLE GOT SAVED?

I MEAN, IF *EVERYONE* HAS INFINITE POTENTIAL FOR *GOOD*, IT SEEMS *UNFAIR* FOR HIM TO SINGLE *SOME* PEOPLE OUT OVER *OTHERS.*

KNOW WHICH UNIVERSE YOU'RE IN *NOW*, SMART-MOUTH?

THE UNIVERSE OF *PAIN!!*

RMD 2005

WAAAAA! WHY GOD? *WHY?*

AMEN!

OBJECTIVELY SPEAKING, ACTION PHILOSOPHER #6 IS:

FRED VAN LENTE TRADED HIS *WRITING* WITH RYAN DUNLAVEY's *DRAWING* (AND VICE-VERSA) TO PRODUCE THIS COMIC BOOK STORY.

IN 1926, TWENTY-ONE-YEAR-OLD SOVIET EMIGRE *ALYSSA ROSENBAUM* ARRIVES IN LOS ANGELES FROM *LENINGRAD* (FORMERLY ST. PETERSBURG) TO FULFILL HER LIFELONG DREAM OF BECOMING A *SCREENWRITER*.

ALYSSA'S FATHER, A BOURGEOIS *PHARMACIST*, WAS *RUINED* BY THE COMMUNIST REVOLUTION WHEN HIS BUSINESS WAS *NATIONALIZED*.

ONE OF ALYSSA'S ONLY MEANS OF ESCAPE FROM HER FAMILY'S HARDSHIPS WAS IN THE *MOVIES*, WHERE SHE WAS *ENRAPTURED* BY AN AMERICA THAT WAS THE EXACT *OPPOSITE* OF THE U.S.S.R.-- WHERE INDIVIDUAL ACHIEVEMENT WAS *REWARDED*, NOT *CONFISCATED*!

UNFORTUNATELY, ALYSSA'S STILL-CREAKY *ENGLISH* PREVENTED HER FROM LANDING A WRITING GIG. BUT SHE MANAGED TO GET AN INTERVIEW WITH HER FAVORITE DIRECTOR, *CECIL B. DE MILLE*, WHO TOOK A SHINE TO THE PLUCKY RUSSIAN HE DUBBED *"CAVIAR."*

DE MILLE GOT ALYSSA A JOB AS AN *EXTRA* ON HIS BIBLICAL EPIC *KING OF KINGS*--THERE SHE FELL IN LOVE WITH ONE OF HER FELLOW BIT PLAYERS, FRANK O'CONNOR. THEY WED IN 1929 AND STAYED MARRIED FOR THE NEXT *FIFTY YEARS!*

TAKING VARIOUS ODD JOBS AROUND THE FILM BUSINESS, ALYSSA STUCK TO HER *WRITING*.

HER FIRST NOVEL, *WE THE LIVING*, AN AUTOBIOGRAPHICAL *ASSAULT* ON THE SOVIET REGIME, WAS PUBLISHED IN 1936. ALYSSA CHANGED HER NAME TO *AYN RAND* TO PROTECT HER FAMILY FROM *REPRISALS* BY THE *K.G.B.*

WE the LIVING
AYN RAND

THE BOOK DID *NOT* SELL WELL. IT DEBUTED IN THE MIDDLE OF THE *GREAT DEPRESSION* AND PRO-SOCIALIST IDEALS WERE IN VOGUE-- PARTICULARLY IN *HOLLYWOOD*.

COMRADE STALIN HAS CREATED A *UTOPIA* FOR THE WORKINGMAN IN RUSSIA--WE IN AMERICA COULD *LEARN* FROM HIM!

PAMPERED, POMPOUS *FOOLS!* THEY'RE JUST SPOUTING THE FANTASIES THEY *WANT* TO BELIEVE! THE BOLSHEVIKS ARE *LOOTERS!*

RAND WAS *DETERMINED* TO PROVIDE AN ALTERNATE VIEW. SHE GOT HER INSPIRATION, IN PART, WHILE WORKING FOR DE MILLE'S *STORY DEPARTMENT* RESEARCHING A (NEVER-PRODUCED) FILM CALLED *THE SKYSCRAPER*.

AFTER INTERVIEWING NUMEROUS *ARCHITECTS*, AND REMEMBERING HOW *AWE-STRUCK* SHE HAD BEEN BY THE SPIRES OF *NEW YORK* THAT HAD BEEN HER FIRST SIGHT OF AMERICA, SHE BEGAN WORK ON A NOVEL, *THE FOUNTAINHEAD* (1943), THAT WOULD OUTLINE NOT JUST A *STORY*, BUT AN ENTIRE *VALUE SYSTEM*.

RAND CALLED THE FUNDAMENTAL PRINCIPLE OF HER *OBJECTIVIST* PHILOSOPHY THE *LAW OF IDENTITY.*

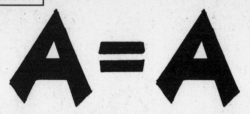

"REALITY -- THE EXTERNAL WORLD -- EXISTS *INDEPENDENT* OF MAN'S CONSCIOUSNESS, INDEPENDENT OF ANY OBSERVER'S KNOWLEDGE, BELIEFS, FEELINGS, DESIRES OR FEARS... THE TASK OF MAN'S CONSCIOUSNESS IS TO *PERCEIVE* REALITY -- *NOT* TO CREATE OR INVENT IT!"

NATURE HAS BESTOWED ON *EVERY* ORGANISM BUT *MAN* INBORN ABILITIES TO SURVIVE IN ITS ENVIRONMENT!

STINGER

TENTACLES

NIGHT VISION

INK

GILLS

FUR

FANGS

CLAWS

PREHENSILE TONGUE

MAN DOES NOT EVEN HAVE THE *INSTINCTS* BEASTS HAVE TO *INNATELY* UNDERSTAND THE WORLD AROUND THEM!

THE *ONLY* TOOLS MAN CAN USE TO *APPREHEND* AND *CONQUER* THE WORLD AROUND HIM ARE THE *JUDGMENTAL* POWERS OF HIS *REASON!*

TO REJECT *REASON* IS TO *DENY* MAN HIS MOST *BASIC* MEANS OF *SURVIVAL!*

TO BE *ANTI-MIND* IS TO BE *ANTI-LIFE!*

TO *ENJOY* THE FRUITS OF ONE'S REASON -- ONE'S OWN *PRODUCTIVE ACHIEVEMENT* --IS THE *MORAL PURPOSE* OF MAN'S LIFE!

IN *THE FOUNTAINHEAD,* ARCHITECT *HOWARD ROARK* SEEKS NOTHING MORE THAN TO REVEL IN THE ACT OF CREATION AND REAP THE REWARDS OF HIS STARTLINGLY ORIGINAL DESIGNS.

BUT HE FINDS HIMSELF *THWARTED* BY "THE HOSTILITY OF SECOND-HAND SOULS" -- INSECURE DEVELOPERS, PIG-HEADED CRITICS, CORRUPT UNIONS -- WHO TRY TO FORCE HIM TO *CONFORM* AND *COMPROMISE!*

THESE **LOOTERS** HAVE BEEN TRYING TO GET PEOPLE TO **SACRIFICE** THEMSELVES FOR "SOCIETY'S" (*I.E.*, *THEIR*) GOOD WITH VARIOUS **JUSTIFICATIONS** AND TO VARIOUS DEGREES OF **EVIL** THROUGHOUT HISTORY!

YOU WILL TURN ALL THE PROFITS OF YOUR PHARMACY OVER TO THE *STATE*, COMRADE ROSENBAUM! IT IS FOR THE GOOD OF THE *PROLETARIAT*!

BECOME AN *ARTIST*? YOU WANT TO *KILL YOUR MOTHER*, HERSCHEL?! NO, YOU'LL BECOME A *DOCTOR*. IT'S FOR THE GOOD OF THE *FAMILY*!

SHOVE THOSE JEWS INTO THE OVENS LIKE YOU WERE *TOLD*, CORPORAL SCHMIDT! IT IS FOR THE GOOD OF THE *WHITE RACE*!

I'M *SORRY* YOUR HUSBAND *BEATS YOU*, MALIKA, BUT YOU MUST SUFFER IN *SILENCE* FOR THE GOOD OF GOD!

THE LOOTERS PERPETUATE THE *LIE* THAT THERE IS NO GREATER VIRTUE THAN *ALTRUISM*-- TO LIVE FOR *OTHERS*, NOT FOR *ONESELF*!

YOU GUYS LIKE ME NOW, RIGHT? HUH? HUH? DO YA? HUH?

BUT THE LOOTERS ARE *HYPOCRITES*! THEY DON'T CARE A WHIT FOR OTHER PEOPLE! AFTER ALL, THEY WANT *YOU* TO SACRIFICE YOURSELF SO *THEY* CAN LIVE!

THE MOST *NAKED* EVOCATION OF LOOTER "VALUES" IS *CHRISTIANITY*!

THEIR *CROSS* REPRESENTS THE *TORTURE* AND *MURDER* OF A SUPERIOR BEING FOR THE SINS OF HIS *INFERIORS*!

HEY.... I'M THE *SON OF GOD*, FOR MY SAKES! WHAT THE HECK AM *I DOIN*'?!

SHE'S GOTTA POINT...

(TO BE FAIR, OBJECTIVISM REJECTS *ALL* RELIGION AS IRRATIONAL *MYSTICISM*.)

I'M GOIN' TO *DISNEYLAND!*

THE LOOTERS ARE A *HOLDOVER* FROM MAN'S *TRIBAL* PAST!

BUT *CIVILIZATION* IS THE PROCESS OF SETTING *MAN* FREE FROM *MEN!*

BOING!

BOING!

BOING!

THE *ONLY* PURPOSE OF *CIVILIZED* GOVERNMENT IS TO PROTECT THE INDIVIDUAL FROM THOSE WHO WOULD *LOOT* THE FRUITS OF HIS REASON BY FORCE OF *ARMS...*

...OR FORCE OF *LAW!*

OOH, BOY! *CRACK MONEY!*

THE ONLY *MORAL* POLITICAL SYSTEM IS *LAISSEZ-FAIRE CAPITALISM!*

HERE MEN ACT AS *EQUAL TRADERS*-- BY FREE, *VOLUNTARY* EXCHANGE TO *MUTUAL* BENEFIT!

THOSE WHO CHOOSE *NOT* TO WORK PRODUCTIVELY NOR USE THEIR REASON SHOULD BE *GRATEFUL* FOR WHAT ALREADY TRICKLES DOWN TO THEM FROM THE THE GREAT CAPITALISTS-- NOT CONTINUOUSLY TRY AND *LOOT* EVEN MORE OF WHAT THEY DID NOT EARN *THEMSELVES!*

GAWRSH, MISTER CAPITALIST SIR, WITHOUT YOUR CREATIONS LIKE *ELECTRICITY* AND *T.V.* I'D STILL BE LIVIN' IN THE *STONE AGE! GOD BLESS* YOU!

JUST DOING WHAT COMES *NATURALLY,* MY GRIMY FRIEND!

IT WOULD TAKE RAND OVER A DECADE TO FINISH HER *NEXT* OBJECTIVIST NOVEL, *ATLAS SHRUGGED*, IN WHICH THE WORLD'S INVENTIVE GENIUSES GO ON *STRIKE* TO CRIPPLE THE ECONOMY RUN BY THOSE WHO UNFAIRLY EXPLOIT THEIR LABOR-- *I.E.*, THE *LOOTERS*.

I AM SO *OUTTA* HERE!

AFTER *ATLAS* WAS PUBLISHED IN 1957, RAND SANK INTO A DEEP *DEPRESSION*. SALES STARTED OUT *SLOW*, AND HER IDEAS WERE PILLORIED BY LIBERALS AND CONSERVATIVES *ALIKE*.

SHE REJECTS *RELIGION*! SHE'S A LEFTIST *RADICAL*!

ALL SHE LOVES IS *MONEY*! SHE'S A RIGHT-WING *FASCIST*!

THE MAN WHO CAME TO HER RESCUE WAS *NATHANIEL BRANDEN*, A CANADIAN-BORN PSYCHIATRIST TWENTY-FIVE YEARS HER *JUNIOR*.

HE HAD BEEN AN ACOLYTE OF AYN'S SINCE HE WAS A STUDENT AT U.C.L.A. AND USED *OBJECTIVISM* IN HIS PRACTICE.

SELF-ESTEEM IS THE CONSEQUENCE OF A MIND FULLY COMMITTED TO *REASON*!

AS SALES OF *ATLAS SHRUGGED* SURGED TO *BESTSELLER* LEVELS, REQUESTS FOR RAND TO *EXPLICATE* HER IDEAS POURED IN FROM AROUND THE COUNTRY. RAND, SELF-CONSCIOUS OF HER THICK *RUSSIAN ACCENT*, HATED PUBLIC SPEAKING. *NATHANIEL*, HOWEVER, EXCELLED AT IT...

...HIS LECTURES IN OBJECTIVSM BECAME *SO* POPULAR HE AND HIS WIFE FOUNDED AN ENTIRE *SCHOOL*--THE NATHANIEL BRANDEN INSTITUTE (N.B.I.)-- *DEVOTED* TO POPULARIZING RAND'S PHILOSOPHY!

BY 1965, N.B.I. OFFERED COURSES IN OBJECTIVISM IN *EIGHTY CITIES* ACROSS NORTH AMERICA.

AMONG ITS INSTRUCTORS WAS RAND ACOLYTE AND FUTURE FEDERAL RESERVE CHAIR *ALAN GREENSPAN*, WHO TAUGHT "THE ECONOMICS OF A FREE SOCIETY."

BY 1967, N.B.I.'S NEWSLETTER, *THE OBJECTIVIST*, HAD OVER 21,000 SUBSCRIBERS! THE OBJECTIVIST REVOLUTION APPEARED WELL UNDER WAY!

RAND CALLED NATHANIEL HER "INTELLECTUAL HEIR." THEY BEGAN A **SEXUAL AFFAIR** IN AN EXEMPLIFICATION OF THE RANDIAN NOTION OF **ROMANTIC LOVE**--

--WHICH IS SIMPLY THE **REASONED** RECOGNITION OF **EQUIVALENT VALUE** IN ANOTHER PERSON!

RAND **INSISTED** SHE AND NATHANIEL CARRY ON THEIR ROMANCE IN **PUBLIC**, SECURING **"CONSENT"** FROM THEIR RESPECTIVE **SPOUSES**.

WHATEVER THE TWO OF YOU MAY BE FEELING, I KNOW YOUR INTELLIGENCE, I KNOW YOU RECOGNIZE THE **RATIONALITY** OF WHAT WE FEEL FOR EACH OTHER...

LIKE MOST **MORALISTS**, RAND PLACED A HIGH VALUE ON **SELF-CONTROL**. ONE OF THE GREATEST ENEMIES OF REASON, SHE SAID, WAS **"EMOTIONALISM."**

"MAN'S EMOTIONAL MECHANISM IS LIKE AN **ELECTRONIC COMPUTER**, WHICH HIS MIND HAS TO **PROGRAM**."

UNFORTUNATELY, NATHANIEL'S OWN SELF-CONTROL LEFT SOMETHING TO BE **DESIRED**. HE SOON EMBARKED ON AN AFFAIR WITH A **THIRD** WOMAN -- AN N.B.I. STUDENT, ACTRESS AND MODEL HIS **OWN AGE**.

THIS IS DOING **WONDERS** FOR MY SELF-ESTEEM!

MINE, TOO!

WHEN RAND FOUND OUT, HER FURY WAS **IMPLACABLE**.

HE **DARES** REJECT ME--**ME**--FOR--FOR A MENTAL **INFERIOR**?!

SHE SUMMONED NATHANIEL TO A MEETING OF OBJECTIVISTS, WHERE HE WAS VIOLENTLY REPUDIATED:

I'LL *DESTROY* YOU AS I *CREATED* YOU! I DON'T EVEN CARE WHAT IT DOES TO *ME*! YOU'LL HAVE *NOTHING*--

--JUST AS YOU *STARTED*, JUST AS YOU CAME TO ME, JUST AS YOU WOULD HAVE REMAINED *WITHOUT ME*!*

*: ACTUAL QUOTE!

IF YOU HAVE AN OUNCE OF MORALITY LEFT *IN* YOU, AN *OUNCE* OF PSYCHOLOGICAL HEALTH--

--YOU'LL BE *IMPOTENT* FOR THE NEXT TWENTY YEARS!

ERROR

RAND MADE SURE NATHANIEL WAS AN ACTIVE PARTICIPANT IN HIS OWN *ANNIHILATION*. HE ADDRESSED THE ENTIRE N.B.I. STUDENT BODY:

I HAVE FAILED TO *PRACTICE* THE PRINCIPLES I TAUGHT TO ALL OF YOU ...

MS. RAND IS FULLY WITHIN HER MORAL RIGHTS IN *SEVERING* OUR RELATIONSHIP...

NATHANIEL WAS FORCED TO CEDE *ALL* INTEREST IN N.B.I. TO RAND HERSELF, AND SHE PROMPTLY *SHUT DOWN* ITS OFFICES-- *SOLD* ALL THE EQUIPMENT AND FURNITURE.

N.B.I.

SHE'D WIPE OUT EVERY *TRACE* OF HER UNFAITHFUL LOVER, EVEN THE INSTITUTE THAT BORE *HIS* NAME -- BUT EXISTED ONLY TO DISSEMINATE *HER* IDEAS!

OBJECTIVISM, AS A COHERENT PHILOSOPHICAL SYSTEM SUPPORTED BY N.B.I., *CEASED TO EXIST!*

RAND LIKED TO SAY THAT MODERN CULTURE "SEEMED TOTALLY INDIFFERENT TO MY IDEAS AND TO IDEAS IN GENERAL."

SHE MADE SURE THAT THAT WOULD BE A *SELF-FULFILLING PROPHECY*.

THE TIME? 1885!

THE *PLACE*? THE *SALPETRIERE CLINIC* IN PARIS, A HOSPITAL FOR *"HYSTERICS"* RUN BY LEGENDARY NEUROLOGIST *JEAN-MARTIN CHARCOT*!

I LOST TOUCH WITH THE *GERMAN* TRANSLATOR OF MY LECTURES AFTER THE *WAR*.

BUT YOUR PAPERS ON *ORGANIC DISEASES* OF THE *NERVOUS SYSTEM* WERE MOST IMPRESSIVE-- ESPECIALLY FOR A *STUDENT*!

YOU SHALL MAKE A FINE REPLACEMENT, *ACTION PHILOSOPHER #7*:

SIGMUND FREUD!

THIS TALE COULDN'T BE REPRESSED BY EITHER... *FRED "SUPER-EGO" VAN LENTE* (SCRIPT) OR *RYAN "ID" DUNLAVEY!* (ARTWORK)

EVER NOTICE HOW *"HYSTERIA"* AND *"HYSTERECTOMY"* SOUND A LOT ALIKE?

THAT'S BECAUSE THEY'RE ROOTED IN THE SAME GREEK WORD -- *HYSTERA*, OR *UTERUS*!

CRAZY NAUGHTY BITS

UP UNTIL THE LATE 19TH CENTURY, IT WAS BELIEVED THAT *MENTAL ILLNESS* ORIGINATED IN THE *WOMB*!

EARLY TREATMENTS INCLUDED *STRAPPING DOWN* THE ABDOMEN TO KEEP A *LOOSE UTERUS* IN PLACE... AND *VAGINAL ENEMAS* OF ICE WATER TO COOL DOWN OVERHEATED GIRL PARTS!

THIS'LL BE A LITTLE *CHILLY*-- ~:OOF!:~

AND THEY CALL *ME* CRAZY!

STILL CONVINCED THAT *HYPNOSIS* WAS THE KEY TO CURING MENTAL ILLNESS, FREUD CORRESPONDED WITH PSYCHIATRISTS LIKE *JOSEF BREUER* WHO USED THE CUTTING-EDGE TECHNIQUE.

I AM TREATING THE MOST *FASCINATING* PATIENT, SIGMUND--SHE'S PRACTICALLY AN *ENCYCLOPEDIA* OF HYSTERICAL SYMPTOMS!

YOUNG *BERTHA PAPPENHEIM* SPENT MUCH OF 1880 AND 1881 OBSESSIVELY CARING FOR HER *INVALID FATHER.* SHE REFUSED TO LEAVE DAD'S BEDSIDE, SPURNING BOTH FOOD AND REST.

HER MENTAL STATE *DETERIORATED* ALONG WITH HER FATHER'S CONDITION, AND WHEN HE FINALLY DIED, HER PSYCHE WENT *KABLOOEY!*

SHE ALTERNATED BETWEEN FITS OF RAGE AND AN UNRESPONSIVE *STUPOR* OR PARTIAL *PARALYSIS.*

SHE HALLUCINATED THAT THE WALLS OF HER ROOM WERE *CRUSHING* HER--

--AND THAT HER *HAIR* WOULD TURN INTO *SNAKES!*

<TO TORMENT, TO TORMENT...>

AT TIMES, SHE COULD ONLY SPEAK IN *INFINITIVES!*

AT OTHERS, WOULD SPEAK ONLY IN *ENGLISH,* NOT HER NATIVE *GERMAN!*

SHE COULD NOT RECOGNIZE HER CLOSEST RELATIVES!

ONCE RIGHT-HANDED, SHE BECAME *LEFT-HANDED!*

SHE WOULD ONLY EAT WHEN BREUER *FED* HER, BUT ALWAYS REFUSED *BREAD!*

!

WHILE *CONSCIOUS*, BERTHA COULD PROVIDE NO *EXPLANATION* FOR HER PSYCHOSES.

BUT WHEN BREUER *HYPNOTIZED* HER, SHE *IMMEDIATELY* MADE CONNECTIONS BETWEEN THE SYMPTOMS AND TRAUMATIC EVENTS THAT HAPPENED TO HER WHILE CARING FOR HER *FATHER*.

"ONCE, I THOUGHT I SAW A *SNAKE* SLITHER UP TO HIS BESIDE... MY *RIGHT HAND* BECAME *PARALYZED* WITH FEAR ... I SUNG AN *ENGLISH* NURSERY RHYME TO *CALM* MYSELF..."

BERTHA'S SYMPTOMS GENERALLY *VANISHED* EACH TIME SHE *DESCRIBED* THEM TO BREUER. SHE CALLED THIS *UNBURDENING* OF HER MIND "CHIMNEY-SWEEPING"; OR, IN A TURN-OF-PHRASE THAT WOULD BECOME *FAMOUS*:

IT'S THE *TALKING CURE!*

MY DEAR *JOSEF*, DO YOU REALIZE WHAT THIS *MEANS*? THERE HAS TO BE A *STOREHOUSE* IN THE MIND FOR EVENTS THE *CONSCIOUS* MIND REFUSES TO ACCEPT-- SOME KIND OF ...

... *UNCONSCIOUS* THAT CAN BE ACCESSED THROUGH HYPNOTISM!

OH ... I THOUGHT SHE WAS JUST *NUTS.*

IN 1895 FREUD AND BREUER PUBLISHED *STUDIES ON HYSTERIA*, WHICH EXPLICATED THE *TALKING CURE* THROUGH BERTHA'S CASE-- RENAMED "ANNA O" IN THE BOOK.

GOTTA *GO!*

WIMP.

STUDIES OF HYSTERIA

THE BOOK WAS *SAVAGED* BY CRITICS--BREUER COULDN'T TAKE THE *HEAT*, LEAVING FREUD TO CONTINUE THEIR RESEARCH *ALONE.*

LESS THAN TWO MONTHS AFTER *STUDIES* APPEARED THE FREUD FAMILY VACATIONED IN *BELLEVUE*, OUTSIDE VIENNA

OTTO STOPPED BY TODAY. HE SAW MY PATIENT "IRMA," AND SAID SHE'S NOT *WELL*--HIS TONE IMPLIED MY TREATMENT HAD *FAILED* HER! THE *NERVE* OF HIM!

EUREKA! MARTHA, *DREAMS* ARE THE *ROYAL ROAD* TO THE *UNCONSCIOUS!*

WHATEVER... -:SNORT!:-

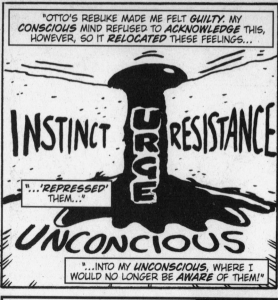

"OTTO'S REBUKE MADE ME FELT *GUILTY.* MY *CONSCIOUS* MIND REFUSED TO *ACKNOWLEDGE* THIS, HOWEVER, SO IT *RELOCATED* THESE FEELINGS..."

INSTINCT **URGE** RESISTANCE

"...'REPRESSED' THEM..."

UNCONCIOUS

"...INTO MY *UNCONSCIOUS,* WHERE I WOULD NO LONGER BE *AWARE* OF THEM!"

"MY DREAM, THEN, WAS *FULFILLMENT* OF MY UNCONSCIOUS WISH TO BE *ABSOLVED* OF MY GUILT ..."

"... IF IRMA'S PROBLEMS WERE *PHYSIOLOGICAL* IN NATURE, I COULD NOT *POSSIBLY* TREAT THEM THROUGH *PSYCHOLOGICAL* MEANS!"

NO LESS SIGNIFICANT WAS THE NON-SEQUITER REFERENCE TO *TRIMETHYLAMIN.* A RESEARCHER OF FREUD'S ACQUAINTANCE BELIEVED THIS ENZYME TO BE A BY-PRODUCT OF *SEXUAL INTERCOURSE.*

AND THE *PHALLIC* IMAGERY OF THE "*DIRTY*" NEEDLE WAS *UNMISTAKABLE!*

IRMA WAS A *YOUNG WIDOW;* HER RELATIVES DESPERATELY WANTED HER TO *REMARRY.* WAS FREUD'S DREAM *ACTUALLY* EXPRESSING HIS *REAL* OPINION ABOUT THE SOURCE OF HER NEUROSES:

BITCH JUST NEEDS TO *GET LAID!*

SOMETHING FREUD WOULD NEVER *SAY--* OR EVEN *THINK--* IN *POLITE* COMPANY?

FREUD COULD NO LONGER IGNORE THE *OBVIOUS FACT* THAT HIS PATIENTS' *REPRESSED THOUGHTS* TENDED TO BE *SEXUAL* IN NATURE.

DADDY AND I ARE JUST *PLAYING,* JUNIOR... -:HEH!:-

OH, YEAH. THIS'LL *SCAR.*

FREUD WROTE "THERE WAS A GREAT DEAL OF *EQUIVOCATION* AND *MYSTERY-MAKING* TO BE OVERCOME, BUT, ONCE THAT HAD BEEN DONE IT TURNED OUT THAT *EVERYTHING* THAT HAD BEEN FORGOTTEN ...

TRAUMA

...HAD IN SOME WAY OR OTHER BEEN EITHER ALARMING OR *PAINFUL* AND *SHAMEFUL* BY THE STANDARDS OF THE SUBJECT'S PERSONALITY."

FREUD PLANNED TO *HYPNOTIZE* HIS PATIENTS INTO *IDENTIFYING* THE PAST EVENT THAT *INSPIRED* THEIR NEUROSES-- THEREBY *CURING* THEM.

OH, HERR *DOKTOR*...

-SNAP!-

BUT THE HYPNOTIC TECHNIQUE HAD *CRIPPLING* LIMITATIONS.

!!!

...HOW CAN I *THANK* YOU FOR *HELPING* ME?!

LUNGE!

OOH! SORRY...TO...UH... INTERRUPT...

"I WAS MODEST ENOUGH NOT TO ATTRIBUTE THE EVENT TO MY OWN IRRESISTIBLE *PERSONAL ATTRACTION*," FREUD SARDONICALLY WROTE LATER.

THE WOMAN WAS TOO *EMBARRASSED* TO BE PUT BACK IN A TRANCE AGAIN, *RUINING* HER FUTURE TREATMENT!

-HEH!- SORRY, DOC, THIS JUST DOESN'T *DO* IT FOR ME ANYMORE...

UH-OH! "THE PERSONAL *EMOTIONAL RELATION* BETWEEN DOCTOR AND PATIENT IS *STRONGER* THAN THE WHOLE CATHARTIC PROCESS!"

FREUD WOULD LATER CALL THIS PHENOMENON *TRANSFERENCE*.

"SO I *ABANDONED* HYPNOTISM, ONLY RETAINING MY PRACTICE OF REQUIRING THE PATIENT TO LIE UPON A SOFA WHILE I SAT *BEHIND* HIM, SEEING HIM BUT NOT *SEEN* MYSELF."

FREUD CALLED HIS NEW METHOD *PSYCHOANALYSIS,* ASKING THE SAME QUESTIONS OF PEOPLE WHEN *NOT* IN A TRANCE, BUT USING FEELINGS OF *TRUST* TO SECURE THEIR COMPLIANCE!

THE TECHNIQUE TOOK A *WHILE* TO CATCH ON. FREUD'S EXPLICATION OF HIS THEORY OF THE UNCONSCIOUS, *THE INTERPRETATION OF DREAMS,* SOLD LESS THAN 300 COPIES WHEN IT PREMIERED IN 1900.

SHOVE!

FREUD'S THEORIES HAD THEIR ADMIRERS, BUT FEW BEYOND HIS SMALL, AND ALMOST EXCLUSIVELY *JEWISH* CIRCLE.

BUT, DISPLAYING HIS LIFELONG *RESILIENCY* IN THE FACE OF *SCORN,* FREUD SOLDIERED *ON.* IN REFINING HIS THEORY OF REPRESSION, FREUD DEVELOPED A *STRUCTURE* OF THE *MIND:*

SUPER EGO · EGO · ID

THE *"SUPER-EGO"* IS THE INTERNALIZATION OF SOCIAL AND FAMILIAL *CENSORSHIP* THAT OPPOSES THE *BLIND URGES* GURGLING UP FROM THE *"ID."*

THE NET RESULT OF THE *TENSION* BETWEEN THESE TWO IS OUR *CONSCIOUSNESS,* OR *"EGO!"*

THE ID'S URGES ARE NEVER *ENTIRELY* BANISHED, HOWEVER. IN *HEALTHY* PEOPLE, THEY MANIFEST THEMSELVES IN *DREAMS,* AND NOT-SO-"ACCIDENTAL" *MISSTATEMENTS...*

MAMA, I'D LIKE YOU TO MEET *JUDY,* MY *MOTHER--*

OH! AH, OF COURSE, I MEAN MY *WIFE* ... ⇥HEH!⇤

...FAMED *"FREUDIAN SLIPS!"*

AS FREUD'S PATIENTS *"FREE ASSOCIATED"* ABOUT EVENTS FURTHER AND FURTHER *BACK* IN THEIR CHILDHOODS, HE BEGAN TO DEVELOP HIS THEORY OF *SEXUALITY.*

SEXUAL DEVELOPMENT BEGINS AT *BIRTH!* INFANTS ARE, AT FIRST, *'POLYMORPHOUSLY PERVERSE--*

--GETTING PLEASURE FROM EVERY PART OF THEIR NEW BODIES!

YEAH, BABY! *YEAH!*

VERY QUICKLY, HOWEVER, THE GROWING CHILD DISPLACES THE ENERGY OF THE *SEXUAL INSTINCTS--* THE *"LIBIDO"--* ONTO *SPECIFIC BODY PARTS.*

IN THE *"ORAL"* STAGE OF DEVELOPMENT, THE CHILD LEARNS THAT *CONSUMING* IS PLEASURABLE--AND BECOMES FIXATED ON THE *MOUTH!*

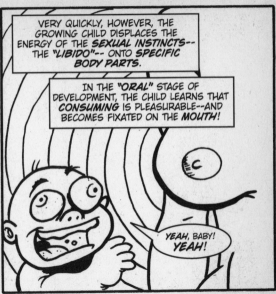

YEAH, BABY! *YEAH!*

HOWEVER, DURING *POTTY-TRAINING,* THE CHILD *ALSO* LEARNS THAT *RETENTION* CAN BE PLEASURABLE-- THIS IS KNOWN AS THE *"ANAL"* STAGE!

NNNGGGGG.... OBVIOUSLY DR. FROOD AIN'T NEVER BEEN *CONSTIPATED...* PLEASURE MY *ASS!* NGGGK!

ONCE A CHILD HITS *PUBERTY,* HE ENTERS THE FINAL, *"GENITAL"* STAGE, IN WHICH THE SEXUAL URGES ARE PROPERLY LOCATED BOTH ON ONE'S OWN BODY-- *AND* THE BODY OF THE *OPPOSITE SEX!*

YEAH, BABY! *YEAH!*

THIS IS THE NATURAL *COURSE* OF THE LIBIDO TO FIND ITS CORRECT *LOVE-OBJECT!*

LIBIDO

LOVE OBJECT

BUT WHEN *SEXUAL TRAUMA* INTERFERES WITH THE LIBIDO'S DEVELOPMENT...

TRAUMA

...*NEUROSES* AND *PERVERSION* CAN RESULT!

YEAH, BABY! *YEAH!*

FOR A SELF-PROCLAIMED MEMBER OF THE "OPPOSITION", FREUD'S SEXUAL VIEWS WERE STRANGELY **CONSERVATIVE.** THE ONLY **"HEALTHY"** OUTLET FOR THE LIBIDO, IN HIS ESTIMATION, WAS **MONOGAMOUS HETEROSEXUALITY...**

...RELEGATING ACTIVITY LIKE MASTURBATION, PROMISCUITY, HOMOSEXUALITY, BISEXUALITY, AND ALL VARIETY OF HARMLESS FETISHES INTO THE CATEGORY OF **"PERVERSION"** FOR **DECADES** TO COME!

THIS WAS, PERHAPS, BECAUSE FREUD BELIEVED A **CERTAIN** DEGREE OF REPRESSION WAS HEALTHY -- IF NOT **MANDATORY!**

YES! YES!

NO! NO!

HE BELIEVED THAT A CHILD **FIRST** FIXATED ITS GENITAL LIBIDO ON THE PARENT OF THE **OPPOSITE SEX** -- AND **REPRESSING** THAT URGE WAS NECESSARY TO NORMAL DEVELOPMENT!

HE CALLED THIS PHENOMENON (IN MALES) THE **"OEDIPUS COMPLEX"**, AFTER THE **GREEK HERO** WHO INADVERTENTLY KILLED HIS FATHER AND MARRIED HIS MOTHER UPON **UNLOCKING** THE RIDDLE OF THE **SPHINX!**

I DON'T KNOW **HOW** I GOT STARTED ON THE WHOLE **RIDDLE** KICK...

AS A **KID** I HAD TO FIGHT REAL HARD WITH THE **GRYPHON** FOR **ATTENTION...**

ANOTHER UNIVERSAL CHILDHOOD SEXUAL EXPERIENCE, ACCORDING TO FREUD, WAS THE CHILD'S DISCOVERY OF THE OTHER GENDER'S **GENITALS:**

WHY DON'T **I** HAVE THAT?

WHAT HAPPENED TO **HERS?!**

FREUD SAID THAT THE **BOY** WOULD ASSUME THAT THE FATHER **CUT OFF** THE GIRL'S PENIS!

THIS **CASTRATION ANXIETY** FORCES THE SON TO **REPRESS** THE OEDIPUS COMPLEX FOR FEAR OF **ANGERING** DADDY!

FOR THE *GIRL'S* PART, HER SELF-ESTEEM IS DAMAGED BY HER *PENISLESSNESS*, WHICH SHE BLAMES ON THE PASSIVE MOTHER.

HMH!

HONEY, *PLEASE* DON'T BE SORE...LOOK, I BOUGHT YOU A *DILDO*...THAT'S *KIND* OF THE SAME THING... ➔*SOB!*◂

FREUD ALSO BELIEVED THIS *"PENIS ENVY"* TURNED THE GIRL AWAY FROM *CLITORAL* SEXUAL SATISFACTION...A STANCE TODAY'S *FEMINISTS* FIND EXCEEDINGLY HARD TO *SWALLOW.*

EVEN FREUD HIMSELF ADMITTED HE WAS *CLUELESS* WHEN IT CAME TO FEMALE SEXUALITY.

I'M *WAY* OUTTA MY LEAGUE HERE...

HE REFERRED TO THE ENTIRE *GENDER* AS "THE *DARK CONTINENT!*"

BUT THE FEMINIST CRITICS WOULD COME *AFTER* FREUD'S DEATH. IN *HIS* DAY, HE WAS ATTACKED AS BEING A *DIRTY OLD MAN*--

--CAPITALIZING ON *PRURIENT* SENSATIONALISM TO SELL BOOKS AND BULK UP HIS PRACTICE.

RIDICULOUS! I AM A *SCIENTIST* AND DEMAND TO BE *TREATED* AS SUCH!

IT'S THIS WIDESPREAD *REFUSAL* TO TALK ABOUT SEXUALITY THAT *CAUSES* MANY NEUROSES IN THE *FIRST* PLACE!

IT LOOKED *UNLIKELY* FREUD'S PSYCHOANALYTIC TECHNIQUE WOULD GAIN ACCEPTANCE UNTIL *1909*, WHEN...

AT *LAST!* THIS COULD BE MY *CHANCE!*

TO BE CONTINUED...

"REMEMBER? YOU TOLD ME YOU DREAMT YOU WERE IN A ROOM OF YOUR HOUSE YOU HAD NEVER *SEEN* BEFORE-- DECORATED WITH THE FURNITURE OF THE *EIGHTEENTH CENTURY!*"

"INTRIGUED, YOU BEGAN EXPLORING, AND FOUND THAT *EACH LEVEL* OF YOUR HOUSE TOOK YOU FURTHER AND FURTHER BACK IN *TIME!*"

"THE LEVEL BENEATH YOUR *CELLAR* LOOKED LIKE A *ROMAN CRYPT!*"

"AT LAST, YOU VENTURED *DEEP* INTO THE HEART OF THE *EARTH...*"

"...AND DISCOVERED SOME KIND OF *PREHISTORIC TOMB* BEFORE WAKING UP!"

WHAT DO YOU THINK IT *MEANS?*

AM I ONE OF YOUR *PATIENTS,* NOW?

BEING ENTIRELY *HONEST* WITH ONESELF IS *GOOD EXERCISE!* WHAT *REPRESSED WISH* DO YOU THINK THE DREAM FULFILLS?

ER...WELL, *YOU'VE* ALWAYS SAID *SKULLS* REPRESENT *DEATH--*

EXACTLY! AND IT IS *MY* DEATH YOU MUST COVET MOST--*YOU* WOULD INHERIT THE MANTLE OF *HEAD* OF OUR MOVEMENT IF I DIED...⇒*HEH!*⇐

I CAN *FEEL...* THE *MURDEROUS WAVES...*EMANATING OFF YOU... OHHH...

THAT'S *RIDICULOUS.* YOU *KNOW* THE LOVE I HAVE FOR YOU, SIG--

NOT *AGAIN.*

THUD!

FREUD WAS *INFAMOUS* FOR FAINTING IN THE PRESENCE OF HIS *MALE* FRIENDS.

WHY DID I MAKE UP THAT PHONY INTERPRETATION OF MY DREAM? I DON'T REALLY *BELIEVE* IT. BUT SIGMUND IS *CONVINCED* THAT *ALL* DREAMS REPRESENT REPRESSED *WISHES...*

...AND HE DEMANDS NOTHING SHORT OF UNWAVERING *LOYALTY* FROM HIS *"CROWN PRINCE"!*

JUNG HAD WON FAME AS THE INVENTOR OF A *PERSONALITY TEST* USED BY PSYCHIATRISTS AROUND THE WORLD; BUT FREUD HAD A MUCH MORE *POLITICAL* MOTIVATION TO DECLARE CARL HIS *"FAVORITE SON":*

HE'S A *GENTILE!* PSYCHOANALYSIS CAN BE CALLED THE *"JEWISH SCIENCE"* NO MORE!

BUT IF FREUD WAS LOOKING FOR A *DUTIFUL LACKEY,* IN CHOOSING THE *FIERCELY INDEPENDENT* JUNG HE HAD MADE A *FATAL ERROR.*

I *LIED* ABOUT MY DREAM TO *PLEASE* SIGMUND! NO ONE MORE THAN *I* SHOULD KNOW BETTER THAN TO DO *THAT!*

HOW MANY *PHONY DIAGNOSES* DOES SIGMUND ELICIT FROM *REGULAR PATIENTS* BECAUSE HE'S *LEADING* THEM *ASTRAY* WITH HIS *RIGID THEORIES*?!

I'M *SURE* HE THINKS I HAVE SOME KIND OF *OEDIPUS* COMPLEX--I'M TRYING TO *"KILL"* AND *OVERTHROW* HIM BECAUSE HE'S MY INTELLECTUAL *"FATHER"!*

"SIGMUND SHOULD ANALYZE *HIMSELF!*

IT'S ALMOST AS IF HE'S USING THE SYMBOLISM OF THE *OEDIPUS* MYTH TO WORK OUT HIS *OWN* FAMILY DRAMAS--

--*WAIT*--

WHAT IF THAT'S WHAT *EVERYONE* DOES?!?

"HE TOLD ME ABOUT HOW HE OFTEN FANTASIZED THAT *PHILIP*--HIS HALF-BROTHER FROM HIS FATHER'S FIRST MARRIAGE--WAS ACTUALLY THE HUSBAND TO HIS *MOTHER,* WHO WAS PHILIP'S AGE!"

SINCE 1901 JUNG HAD BEEN TREATING BANK MESSENGER *EMILE SCHWYZER* FOR DELUSIONS - ONE OF WHICH WAS THAT HE COULD SEE AN ENORMOUS *PENIS* EMANATING FROM THE *SUN!*

IF I *SQUINT* LIKE THIS AND MOVE MY *HEAD* LIKE THIS, THE *SOLAR PHALLUS* PRODUCES THE *WEATHER!*

O-KAAAAY... NUTJOB.

HEEEEY! WHO YOU CALLIN' A *NUTJOB,* PISAN?

HEH - NO OFFENSE *INTENDED,* MR. *MITHRAS,* SIR-- --GULP!

LATER, JUNG WAS *STUNNED* TO DISCOVER THAT SCHWYZER -- A GRAMMAR SCHOOL *DROPOUT* -- WAS EVOKING IMAGERY ALMOST IDENTICAL TO THE LITURGY OF *MITHRAS* -- THE *FERTILITY/SUN GOD* AT THE CENTER OF THE LAST GREAT *PAGAN* RELIGION OF THE ROMAN EMPIRE!

I *SCOURED* EMILE'S MEDICAL HISTORY -- THERE WERE NO *LIBRARIES* IN ANY OF THE PLACES WHERE HE WAS INSTITUTIONALIZED! IF THERE'S NO WAY HE COULD HAVE *LEARNED* THE ANCIENT RITES...

...IT COULD BE A UNIVERSALLY *HUMAN* CHARACTERISTIC TO PRODUCE THE *SAME* IDEAS, AGAIN AND AGAIN!

JUNG'S NEO-*PLATONIC* THEORY CALLED THESE UNIVERSAL PSYCHICAL FORMS *"ARCHETYPES"*...

HERO

...AND, IN A *MAJOR* BREAK FROM FREUD, THE PLACE FROM WHICH THEY EMANATED, THE *"COLLECTIVE UNCONSCIOUS!"*

AFTER ALL, JUNG WROTE, "CONSCIOUSNESS IS A VERY *RECENT* ACQUISITION OF NATURE..."

OOH! OOH!

"...AND IT IS STILL IN AN *EXPERIMENTAL* STATE!"

WHAT IF THE *UNCONSCIOUS* IS JUST AS ACTIVE AS THE *CONSCIOUS* MIND?

EXCEPT THAT WHILE CONSCIOUSNESS REACTS TO *ACTIVE* EXTERNAL STIMULI--

--THE UNCONSCIOUS REGISTERS *SUBLIMINAL*, *EMOTIONAL* IMPULSES FOR WHICH THERE IS NO *ROOM* IN CONSCIOUSNESS!

"THE GENERAL FUNCTION OF *DREAMS* IS TO TRY TO RESTORE OUR *PSYCHOLOGICAL BALANCE* BY PRODUCING DREAM MATERIAL THAT RE-ESTABLISHES, IN A *SUBTLE* WAY, THE *TOTAL PSYCHIC EQUILIBRIUM.*"

"THUS, A DREAM *CANNOT* PRODUCE A DEFINITE THOUGHT. IF IT BEGINS TO DO SO, IT *CEASES* TO BE A DREAM BECAUSE IT CROSSES THE THRESHOLD OF *CONSCIOUSNESS!*"

BUT: "ELEMENTS *OFTEN* OCCUR IN A DREAM THAT ARE *NOT* INDIVIDUAL AND THAT *CANNOT* BE DERIVED FROM THE DREAMER'S *PERSONAL EXPERIENCE.*"

THESE *PRIMORDIAL IMAGES* HAVE BEEN INHERITED BY MAN FROM THE *FIRST DAYS* OF (UN)CONSCIOUSNESS!

IN *ANCIENT TIMES*, THE HUMAN PSYCHE WAS MORE *RECONCILED* TO THESE SEEMINGLY *INEXPLICABLE* IMAGES AND IMPULSES.

WHILE UNFOUNDED *SUPERSTITION* MAY HAVE BEEN PERVASIVE, HUMANS SIMPLY *ACCEPTED* THAT THEY WERE SURROUNDED BY FORCES THEY COULD NEITHER *UNDERSTAND* NOR *CONTROL*!

OUR MODERN-DAY DEPENDENCE ON *SCIENCE*, ON THE OTHER HAND, HAS GIVEN US AN *ILLUSORY* SENSE OF *OMNIPOTENCE* THAT HAS LEFT US *ALIENATED* FROM THE MANIFESTATIONS OF THE COLLECTIVE UNCONSCIOUS! JUNG WRITES:

"MODERN MAN DOES NOT UNDERSTAND HOW MUCH HIS *'RATIONALISM'* (WHICH HAS DESTROYED HIS CAPACITY TO RESPOND TO NUMINOUS SYMBOLS AND IDEAS) HAS PUT HIM AT THE MERCY OF THE PSYCHIC *'UNDERWORLD'*!"

THE *RESULT*? WIDESPREAD *NEUROSIS*!

"OF *COURSE*! THE MEANING OF MY DREAM IS SO *CLEAR*, NOW!"

"I AM LEAVING THE 18TH CENTURY PHILOSOPHERS OF MY SCHOOLING ... THE *MEDIEVAL* IDEAS OF MY PASTOR PARENTS ..."

"MY *DESTINY* IS TO GO AS FAR BACK IN TIME AS I *CAN*--TO PLUMB THE FURTHEST DEPTHS OF THE UNCONSCIOUS *ITSELF*!"

"IT'S *MY* DREAM, ABOUT *MY* LIFE AND *MY* WORLD! IT CAN ONLY BE INTERPRETED *BY* ME!"

*: ACTUAL EXCHANGE!

80

THE RIFT BETWEEN THEM ONLY *WORSENED* UPON THEIR RETURN FROM AMERICA.

"THE PSYCHIC DEVELOPMENT OF THE *INDIVIDUAL* IS A SHORT REPETITION OF THE COURSE OF DEVELOPMENT OF THE *RACE*."

NO! "THE INDIVIDUAL IS THE *ONLY* REALITY. THE FURTHER WE MOVE... TOWARD *ABSTRACT* IDEAS ABOUT *HOMO SAPIENS*, THE MORE LIKELY WE ARE TO FALL INTO *ERROR!*"

FREUD'S THEORIES SOON BECAME THE *WORLDWIDE STANDARD* IN PSYCHOLOGY!

BY 1912, HOWEVER, FREUD AND JUNG HAD STOPPED *SPEAKING*. THE FINAL BREAK BETWEEN TWO OF THE 20TH CENTURY'S GREATEST *GENIUSES* WAS DISHEARTENINGLY *JUVENILE*:

NONETHELESS, FREUD'S *"CLARK LECTURES"*, PUBLISHED IN ENGLISH AS *FIVE LECTURES ON PSYCHOANALYSIS* (1910), BECAME THE *TURNING POINT* IN THE TECHNIQUE'S ACCEPTANCE!

JUNG WAS *INSULTED* THAT FREUD VISITED A *SICK FRIEND* IN *KREUZLINGEN*, SWITZERLAND, AND DID NOT STOP BY TO SEE *HIM*.

THE JUNGS

JUNG'S BRANCH OF THE DISCIPLINE BECAME KNOWN AS *ANALYTICAL PSYCHOLOGY* AND HE GATHERED HIS *OWN* FOLLOWERS. THEY AND THE *FREUDIANS* ENGAGED IN VICIOUS *INTELLECTUAL TURF WARS* THAT CONTINUE TO *THIS DAY!*

THE FREUDIANS CONSTANTLY *ATTACKED* JUNG FOR HIS ALLEGED *MYSTICISM*-- HE TURNED OUT PAPER AFTER PAPER ON THE *"PSYCHIC UNDERWORLD"*:

THE OCCULT ... ALCHEMY ... PARAPSYCHOLOGY ... JUNG EVEN THOUGHT *UFO'S* WERE MANIFESTATIONS OF THE *COLLECTIVE UNCONSCIOUS!*

STILL, HE ATTRACTED A LONG LIST OF FAMOUS AND WEALTHY PATIENTS. *MARY MELLON*, WIFE TO THE HEIR OF THE MELLON *FINANCIAL FORTUNE*, FOUNDED A *NON-PROFIT PUBLISHER* TO RELEASE THE JUNG CAREER *OEUVRE* IN AMERICA!

I'M CALLING IT THE *BOLLINGEN FOUNDATION*, AFTER YOUR *TOWER* ON *LAKE ZURICH!*

THUS ENSURING THE BATTLE BETWEEN THE FREUDIANS & THE JUNGIANS WOULD GO ON...AND ON... AND ON...

THOUGH MARY MELLON CREATED HER *BOLLINGEN FOUNDATION* PRIMARILY TO PUBLISH THE WORKS OF *CARL G. JUNG* IN ENGLISH, IT ALSO BROUGHT OUT BOOKS COVERING THE WHOLE RANGE OF THE FAMED ANALYTICAL PSYCHOLOGIST'S *"COLLECTIVE UNCONSCIOUS!"*

IN FACT, THE PUBLISHER'S *FIRST* BOOK WAS A COMMENTARY ON A *NAVAJO WAR CEREMONY* EDITED BY AN OBSCURE LECTURER AT AN UPSTATE *GIRLS'* COLLEGE.

BOLLINGEN WOULD LIKE TO DO A MODERN-DAY *"BULLFINCH'S MYTHOLOGY"* AND WE THINK *YOU'D* BE THE PERFECT MAN TO WRITE IT, *ACTION PHILOSOPHER #9...*

OUR STORYTELLING PANTHEON CONSISTS OF: *FRED VAN LENTE* LORD OF THE *WRITERLY* HEAVENS *RYAN DUNLAVEY* JANITOR OF THE *ARTISTIC* UNDERWORLD

...JOSEPH CAMPBELL!

JOE CAMPBELL WAS BORN IN *NEW YORK CITY* IN 1904.

WHEN HE WAS SIX, HIS FATHER TOOK HIM TO SEE BUFFALO BILL CODY'S *WILD WEST SHOW* AT *MADISON SQUARE GARDEN.*

THUS BEGAN A LIFELONG FASCINATION WITH *NATIVE AMERICAN* MYTHOLOGY AND FOLKLORE.

JOE *DEVOURED* EVERY BOOK ON AMERICAN INDIANS IN THE CHILDREN'S SECTION OF HIS LOCAL LIBRARY BY THE AGE OF *TEN*...THEN STARTED IN ON THE *ADULT* STACKS!

IT TOOK THE INTELLECTUALLY *RESTLESS* CAMPBELL QUITE A WHILE TO FIGURE OUT WHAT HE WANTED TO *DO* WITH HIS LIFE!

HE PLAYED IN A *JAZZ BAND*... COLLECTED *TIDAL FAUNA* IN ALASKA... WENT *SURFING* IN HAWAII...GOT A FELLOWSHIP TO STUDY MEDIEVAL *FRENCH* AT THE UNIVERSITY OF *PARIS*!

ANYWHERE BUT HERE

HE RETURNED FROM EUROPE JUST IN TIME FOR THE *STOCK MARKET CRASH* OF 1929.

WALL ST.

5¢

OOPS. BAD *TIMING.*

JOBS BEING SCARCE, HE TOOK THE EARNINGS FROM HIS *JAZZ BAND* AND RENTED A CABIN IN *WOODSTOCK* WITH HIS SISTER, AND DID NOTHING BUT *READ* FOR AN ENTIRE YEAR!

?

AT LAST, IN 1934, HE ACCEPTED A TEACHING POSITION AT *SARAH LAWRENCE*, A NEWLY FOUNDED ALL-WOMEN'S *COLLEGE* IN BRONXVILLE, N.Y.

HE REMAINED ONE OF THE MOST POPULAR PROFESSORS IN ITS *LITERATURE* DEPARTMENT FOR THE NEXT THIRTY-EIGHT YEARS!

IN 1941 HE MET JUNG'S CLOSE FRIEND *HEINRICH ZIMMER*, THE FAMED *INDOLOGIST*, WHO RECOMMENDED HIM TO MARY MELLON AND BOLLINGEN.

AFTER ZIMMER'S DEATH IN 1943, MELLON ASKED CAMPBELL TO EDIT THE SCHOLAR'S POSTHUMOUS WRITINGS. HE BECAME *IMMERSED* IN INDIAN MYTHOLOGY!

HE ALSO ASSISTED SWAMI NIKHILANAND IN A NEW ENGLISH TRANSLATION OF *THE UPANISHADS* ("TO SIT CLOSE TO"), THOSE HINDU TREATISES ON THE NATURE OF *MAN* AND THE *UNIVERSE* THAT DATE TO THE *EIGHTH CENTURY B.C.!*

HINDU MYTHOS

ONE OF THE CENTRAL TEACHINGS OF THE *CHHANDOGYA UPANISHAD* IS *TAT TVAM ASI*:

"THOU ART THAT."

THE MYSTERY OF *YOUR* EXISTENCE IS THE *SAME* MYSTERY AS THE MYSTERY OF THE EXISTENCE OF THE UNIVERSE *ITSELF!*

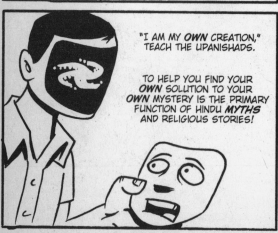

"I AM MY *OWN* CREATION," TEACH THE UPANISHADS.

TO HELP YOU FIND YOUR *OWN* SOLUTION TO YOUR *OWN* MYSTERY IS THE PRIMARY FUNCTION OF HINDU *MYTHS* AND RELIGIOUS STORIES!

"MY DISTINCT IMPRESSION THROUGHOUT WAS THAT I WAS AT WORK ONLY ON SEPARATE *CHAPTERS* OF A *SINGLE MYTHOLOGICAL EPIC* OF THE HUMAN IMAGINATION!"

CAMPBELL WAS ALSO INFLUENCED BY THE WORK OF 19TH CENTURY ETHNOLOGIST *ADOLF BASTIAN.*

BASTIAN TERMED THE SIMILARITIES BETWEEN WORLD MYTHOLOGIES *"ELEMENTARY IDEAS"*...

...AND THEIR INDIVIDUAL MANIFESTATIONS IN DIFFERENT CULTURES THROUGHOUT HISTORY, *"ETHNIC IDEAS!"*

TAKE *THIS* RELIGIOUS FIGURE, WHO WAS BORN OF A *VIRGIN*...

EMPLOYED SUCH RITES AS *BAPTISM*, THE DRINKING OF *WINE*, AND THE BREAKING OF *BREAD*...

WAS SYMBOLIZED BY A *CROSS*...

AND CELEBRATED HIS *BIRTHDAY* ON DECEMBER 25!

IF YOU SAID *MITHRAS*, FERTILITY GOD OF THE LATE ROMAN EMPIRE, YOU'D *ALSO* BE RIGHT!

HEEEEY! HOW'S IT *HANGIN'*, PISAN?

YOU WANNA SEE ME MAKE IT *SNOW* WITH MY *PENIS*?

UH... NO.

OF COURSE, TWO *IMMACULATE CONCEPTIONS* ARE NOTHING TO GET EXCITED ABOUT. THE VIRGIN BIRTH IS ONE OF THE MOST *ELEMENTARY* ELEMENTARY IDEAS OF THEM ALL, FOUND NOT JUST IN THE STORIES OF MITHRAS AND *JESUS*...

...BUT DEGANAWIDA, THE *GREAT PEACEMAKER* OF THE *IROQUOIS*...

...AND THE *BUDDHA*, WHO WAS SAID TO HAVE DESCENDED FROM HEAVEN INTO HIS MOTHER'S WOMB IN THE FORM OF A *MILK-WHITE ELEPHANT!*

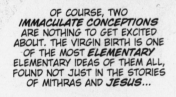

WHAT? YOU'D DARE COMPARE THE GREAT *WORLD RELIGIONS* TO THOSE...*MYTHS*?!

"FROM THE POINT OF VIEW OF ANY *ORTHODOXY*, MYTH MIGHT BE DEFINED SIMPLY AS '*OTHER PEOPLE'S RELIGION*'...

"...TO WHICH AN EQUIVALENT DEFINITION OF *RELIGION* WOULD BE '*MISUNDERSTOOD MYTHOLOGY!*'"

MISUNDERSTAND *THIS*, BLASPHEMER!

OKAY... IT'S *YOUR* FUNERAL!

WAAAAIT... WHAT DO YOU MEAN *MY* FUNERAL?

HUMANITY HAS NOT BEEN HISTORICALLY *FORGIVING* TO RELIGIONS THAT REMAIN GLUED TO THEIR *ETHNIC IDEAS*!

"WHEN THE AMERICANS DESTROYED THEIR WAY OF LIFE, THE PLAINS INDIANS EXPERIENCED A *SPIRITUAL* APOCALYPSE AS THEIR MYTHS FAILED THEM!"

"THEIR PRAYERS WENT *UNHEEDED*, AND A ONCE-PROUD PEOPLE DEGENERATED INTO POVERTY AND *SUBSTANCE ABUSE*!"

LIKEWISE, THE MONOTHEISTIC RELIGIONS OF THE MIDDLE EAST --CHRISTIANITY, ISLAM AND JUDAISM-- INSIST THAT THEIR MYTHS ARE NOT *METAPHORICAL*, BUT *LITERAL TRUTH*!

THESE "*RELIGIONS OF THE BOOK*" RESIST CHANGE AT EVERY TURN, EVEN AS THE WORLD OF *SCIENCE* CHANGES AROUND THEM!

THE FUTURE

OUR MODERN WORLD HAS SPLIT BETWEEN TRIBAL *FUNDAMENTALISM*....

GOD LIKES *ME*!

NO HE DOESN'T! HE LIKES *ME*!

DOES NOT!

DOES TOO!

...AND SECULAR *INDIFFERENCE*!

~GULP!~

CHURCH ATTENDANCE

WESTERN MAN APPEARS TO BE DOING TO *HIMSELF* WHAT HE DID TO THE NATIVE AMERICANS!

HE IS CAUGHT BETWEEN TWO FORCES THAT INSIST ON BEING THE SOLE ARBITERS OF *ABSOLUTE TRUTH!*

SCIENCE DOES *NOTHING* FOR MAN SPIRITUALLY, AND *ORGANIZED RELIGION* DEMANDS BLIND FAITH IN AN ILLOGICAL LITURGY THAT *WAS NEVER MEANT TO BE TAKEN LITERALLY!*

SCIENCE

RELIGION

WHICH TAKES US BACK TO WHERE WE *BEGAN* THIS TALE:

BULLFINCH'S HAS BEEN *DONE.* I'D MUCH RATHER DO A BOOK THAT EXPLAINS HOW TO *READ* A MYTH.

YOU MEAN LIKE A *SELF-HELP* BOOK?

ER... *SURE.*

GO FOR IT!

IT TOOK CAMPBELL ALMOST *FIVE YEARS* TO CREATE A BOOK-LENGTH EXPLICATION OF HIS IDEA OF A *MONOMYTH* (A TERM BORROWED FROM JAMES JOYCE)-- A TALE THAT VARIES IN THE TELLING FROM CULTURE TO CULTURE...

JOSEPH CAMPBELL
THE HERO WITH A THOUSAND FACES

...BUT REMAINS, IN ITS *SPIRITUAL* ASPECTS, THE *SAME* STORY!

THE HERO'S JOURNEY IS A *METAPHOR* FOR EACH INDIVIDUAL'S TRANSFORMATION OF *CONSCIOUSNESS!*

THE DIFFERENT *PLACES* VISITED ON THE ADVENTURE REPRESENT DIFFERENT STATES OF *MIND!*

THE ULTIMATE BOON IS THE REVELATION WE ARE *ALL* CHRIST--WE ARE *ALL* BUDDHA--WE ARE *ALL* MITHRAS!

"TAT TVAM ASI!"

SALE

AS HEINRICH ZIMMER WROTE, "FOR INDIAN ART, MAN *IS* GOD."

"ART IS CREATED SO THAT HE MIGHT EXPERIENCE THIS TRUTH ... AND *NEED ART NO LONGER!*"

MYTHS, LEGENDS AND STORIES ARE THE *SIGNPOSTS* PREVIOUS GENERATIONS HAVE LEFT US SO WE DON'T HAVE TO FIGURE OUT OUR OWN PERSONAL JOURNEY IN *SOLITUDE!*

THEY *HAVE* TO BE METAPHORICAL, BECAUSE THEIR INTERPRETATION WILL BE DIFFERENT FOR EACH *INDIVIDUAL* LIFE!

INSTRUCTIONS

LiFE

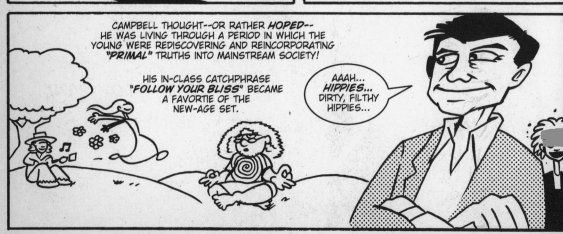

CAMPBELL THOUGHT--OR RATHER *HOPED*--HE WAS LIVING THROUGH A PERIOD IN WHICH THE YOUNG WERE REDISCOVERING AND REINCORPORATING *"PRIMAL"* TRUTHS INTO MAINSTREAM SOCIETY!

HIS IN-CLASS CATCHPHRASE *"FOLLOW YOUR BLISS"* BECAME A FAVORTIE OF THE NEW-AGE SET.

AAAH... HIPPIES... DIRTY, FILTHY HIPPIES...

IN *PSYCHOLOGY*, THE FUNCTION OF MYTHOLOGY IS TO CARRY TO INDIVIDUAL OVER THE THRESHOLDS OF GROWTH, FLOWERING AND *DECLINE.*

HUMANS, AFTER ALL, HAVE THE LONGEST *INFANCY* OF ANY ANIMAL ON EARTH-- NEARLY *TWELVE YEARS* PASS BEFORE A PERSON CAN *CONTEMPLATE* INDEPENDENCE FROM ADULTS!

A NEUROTIC, IT MIGHT BE SAID, IS A PERSON WHOSE *SPONTANEOUS REACTION* IS ONE OF *DEPENDENCY* LONG AFTER THE TRANSFORMATION INTO *ADULTHOOD* SHOULD HAVE OCCURRED!

LEAP!

AAHH! SNAKES!

CAMPBELL THEORIZED THAT THE FUNCTION OF *FREUDIAN PSYCHOANALYSIS* WAS THE SAME AS THE *PUBESCENT INITIATION RITE* IN PRIMAL CULTURES: TRANSFORMING THE PSYCHOLOGY OF THE CHILD BY USING THE APPROPRIATE *MYTHS!*

THE STORY OF *OEDIPUS* MIGHT HELP EXPLAIN YOUR FEELINGS ABOUT YOUR *MOTHER...*

HUMANS ALSO HAVE THE LONGEST *OLD AGE* OF ANY ANIMAL! CARL JUNG FAMOUSLY SAID THAT HIS *ANALYTICAL PSYCHOLOGY* COULD REALLY ONLY HELP PEOPLE OVER THE AGE OF *THIRTY-FIVE!*

I MIGHT SUGGEST THAT THE *ARCHETYPE* YOU'RE STRUGGLING WITH IS THAT OF THE *ANIMUS...*

...ONE THINKS OF THE LEGENDARY SEER *TIRESIAS*, WHO WAS BOTH MAN *AND* WOMAN...

SO YOU *SEE?* YOUR TWO THEORIES ARE REALLY THE *SAME*, JUST APPLIED TO *DIFFERENT* STAGES OF THE HERO'S JOURNEY!

HE'S *RIGHT!* ->SOB!<- I'M SO SORRY WE *FOUGHT*, CARL!

ME TOO!

I LOVE YOU, SIGGY!! ->SNIFFLE!<-

(OH, UH... THIS NEVER *HAPPENED.*)

about the creators

Ryan Dunlavey

has studied illustration, fine art and creative writing at Syracuse University and animation at the School of Visual Arts. He currently lives in Brooklyn (*"Where the weak are killed and eaten!"*) slugging out a living as a two-fisted freelance illustrator, animator and graphic design jack-of-all trades. His clients past and present include Disney, Warner Bros., Scholastic, Penguin, McGraw-Hill, The Princeton Review, Classic Media, Comedy Central, Nickelodeon, MTV, PBS, ABC News, Central Park, Time Out, Airwalk, The Children's Place, American Greetings and *both* the WCW and WWF.

Ryan's comics have appeared in *MAD, Royal Flush, ToyFare* and *Wizard* magazines and has self-published comics for over a decade, including the series *Evil Twin* and *Tommy Atomic*.

Bask in his simple goodness at his web site, *http://www.ryandeluxe.com Bask damn you!!!*

Fred Van Lente

holds a B.A., with Honors, in English and Textual Studies from Syracuse University, although no one really explained to him what "English and Textual Studies" really means. A proud graduate school dropout, after teaching writing at the University of Pittsburgh he decided death was preferable to academia. He was too chicken to kill himself, though, so he did the next best thing: He moved to Brooklyn and began a career writing comics.

Fred's graphic novels include *Scorpion: Poison Tomorrow* (Marvel), *The Silencers* (Image/Moonstone) and *Tranquility* (1998 winner of a Spectrum Award for Best Science Fiction Art).

Fred is proud to serve as Head Curator and Secretary of the Board at *MoCCA*, the Museum of Comic and Cartoon Art in New York City (*http://www.moccany.org*)

Anyone who can explain to him what his degree means is encouraged to contact him through his official web site, *http://www.fredvanlente.com*.